W9-BUX-395

Help Your Child to Read and Write

Expert advice from:
Professor Rhona Stainthorp, BA, MSc, PhD, PGCE, AFBPS, CPsychol
Institute of Education, University of Reading

Dr Matthew Saxton, MA, MSc, DPhil
Institute of Education, University of London

Cover design by Mary Cartwright
and Joanne Kirkby

Help Your Child to Read and Write

Fiona Chandler

Illustrated by Shelagh McNicholas
and Ruth Russell

Designed by Claire Ever

Edited by Felicity Brooks

Additional material by Nicola Hall

Contents

Babies and toddlers (0 – 2½ years)

Preschoolers (2½ – 4 years)

Beginner readers (4 – 7 years)

Young readers (7 – 11 years)

Useful information

Introduction

Reading and writing are among the most vital skills a child can learn. They're essential if children are to make good progress at school and eventually take their place in the wider world. Research shows that parents can have a huge impact on their children's literacy skills – and the sooner you start the better. From the earliest years of life, you can provide valuable experiences that will give your child a head start when they begin school.

Did you know?

Helping with your child's reading and writing has a bigger effect on their success at school than your level of education, job or income.

Children who start school with a love of books are more likely to become good readers.

Learning to read shouldn't be a chore – it's really important that children learn to love books too.

Reading to children and talking about books together helps them to become better readers and writers.

In this book, you'll find lots of practical ideas to help prepare children for learning to read and write, as well as advice on how to support them once they start school. The book is divided into sections according to age, but bear in mind that children develop at different rates and some may progress slightly faster or slower than others.

One of the most important things you can do is to be enthusiastic about reading, so children see it as useful and fun. Whenever possible, let them see you reading – anything from newspapers and books to recipes and road signs. Above all, open your child's eyes to the exciting world of stories by looking at books and reading together. Once children are hooked, reading will be a source of pleasure, as well as a vital skill, for the rest of their lives.

Babies and toddlers

It sounds incredible, but from the moment children are born, they start to develop skills they will eventually need for reading and writing. One of the first steps on the road to becoming a reader is learning to talk, and this process starts long before toddlers say their first words. You can help your baby to develop good language skills by talking, singing, playing and reading together.

Key skills at a glance

Interacting with other children and adults

Recognizing and paying attention to different sounds

Making a range of sounds and gestures and using these to communicate

Understanding words and sentences

Saying words and short sentences

Taking part in conversations

Becoming familiar with books, songs and rhymes

Making marks, squiggles and scribbles

0 – 2½ years

Talking to babies

Babies are able to listen and communicate from the day they're born. In fact, research shows that they can actually hear and recognize their mother's voice while they're still in the womb. It may seem strange talking to someone who can't talk back, but your baby will love hearing your voice – and will learn how to talk by listening to you.

Talking to even tiny babies helps them learn the rhythms and patterns of speech, so try to talk to your baby as often as you can. It helps if you speak in a lively voice and make eye contact as you chat. People often talk to babies in a high-pitched, sing-song voice, and studies show that babies actually prefer this way of talking to adult speech.

Everyday routines, such as dressing, feeding, changing and bathing, are great opportunities to talk. Throughout the day, describe what you're doing and what will happen next, for example, 'Time for your bath. Let's take off your T-shirt!' Linking words with actions like this helps your baby to learn what the words mean. You can talk to babies about anything they can see, touch or hear.

Ideas for talking to babies

- Point out interesting things that you pass in the street or in the park.
- Help babies to learn names by saying them often, for example, 'Here's Granny.'
- Point out sounds you hear, for example, 'There's the doorbell ringing.'
- When you give a baby an object, say clearly what it is, for example, 'Here's your cup.'

Babies who are spoken to a lot have a bigger vocabulary by the time they are two.

Chatting and playing

Babies need to learn that when people talk to each other, they take it in turns to speak. You can teach them this by answering when they coo, gurgle or babble. Babies as young as three months old will often wait for a response after they have 'said' something. If they 'say' something else, wait for them to finish and then reply.

Babies love hearing things repeatedly; it makes the world seem more familiar and helps them to learn. Simple games, such as those on the right, are a great way to practise the same speech patterns over and over again. You can play a game many times before a baby tires of it.

Talking games

- Hide your face behind your hands, then pop back into view, exclaiming 'Peek-a-boo, I see you!'
- Hide a favourite toy behind your back and ask 'Where's Teddy?' Then produce Teddy, exclaiming 'Here he is!'
- Stand in front of a mirror. Ask 'Where's Ben's mouth?' Point and say 'Here's Ben's mouth.' Repeat with other body parts.

You can encourage babies to 'talk' more by smiling, making eye contact and sounding enthusiastic about what they 'say.'

Useful tip

You can learn new songs and rhymes by borrowing rhyming books and CDs from the library.

Rhyme time

Singing songs and reciting nursery rhymes to babies is a great way to boost their language development. By listening to rhymes again and again, your baby learns to tune into the regular sounds and rhythms of the language. Babies soon begin to recognize their favourite rhymes and enjoy knowing what will come next. Singing can be lots of fun for you both, especially if you use rhymes with actions, such as 'Round and round the garden'.

It helps if you look at the baby as you sing, emphasize rhyming words and tap your feet, or clap, in time to the beat.

Learning to talk

It's good to have special times in the day for one-to-one 'conversations' away from any background noise.

There is a strong link between language development and learning to read and write – children who start school with poor language skills are more likely to have problems with reading. Fortunately, there are lots of ways to help young children develop good language skills. Babies and toddlers naturally learn language, so they don't have to be taught – they just need lots of opportunities to talk and listen.

Children learn how to talk by imitating the speech sounds they hear around them. The first sounds babies make are usually 'ooh', 'oh' or 'aah' noises. Then, from about eight months, they start to say recognizable syllables, such as 'ba', 'ma', 'da' and 'ga'. When they string these together to make repeated sounds, such as 'mamamama' or 'babababa', it's called babbling.

Babies' babbling often sounds like real speech, because they copy the rhythms and tones of the voices they hear.

Helping with first words

- Use actions and gestures to show what words mean, such as 'Wave bye-bye!'
- Name objects that babies see around them, e.g. toys, clothes or parts of the body.
- If a baby tries to say a word, smile and say 'That's right!', then say it back correctly.

First words

Most babies say their first words at around 10 to 14 months. These are words they will have heard many, many times before, usually the names of familiar people or objects. As babies babble, they may say words like 'mama' and 'dada' accidentally, and only learn what they mean when people react to them. At this stage, babies start to repeat parts of words that they hear and may even make up their own names for things. This is completely normal and nothing to worry about.

Toddler talk

By 18 months, toddlers may be able to say about 50 different words, though they won't always pronounce them properly. They often use single words to mean whole sentences, so the word 'mo' may mean 'I want more juice.'

At 18 to 24 months, many toddlers put on a 'word spurt', learning lots of new words very quickly. They start saying short, two-word phrases, such as 'Daddy gone'. At first, they only know a few set phrases, but soon they learn to put words together to invent their own combinations. Children learn language at different rates, so don't panic if your toddler seems slow to talk. Some toddlers don't say a recognizable word until they're two and a half.

Tips for talking to toddlers

- Use short sentences and ask lots of questions.
- Give toddlers your full attention when they're talking to you.
- Be patient – it can take time for toddlers to sort out what they want to say.
- Answer toddlers' questions as simply as you can.
- Praise your toddler's attempts to talk and never criticize or laugh at them.

Talking to toddlers

Toddlers like it if you talk to them in a lively way about things that interest them. As they play, talk about what they're doing and ask simple questions, for example 'What's Teddy doing?' or 'Where's the red car?' Make the most of everyday activities, such as shopping, by pointing things out, explaining what you're doing and getting your toddler involved, for example in spotting items at the supermarket.

Toddlers learn best by having real conversations, so it's important to listen and respond enthusiastically when they talk. Don't worry if they make a mistake – just repeat back what they've said using the right words. It helps if you expand on what they say, so if a toddler says 'Big dog', you could reply 'That *is* a big dog. Look, he's wagging his tail.'

Toddlers often use gestures, along with words, to make themselves understood.

Encouraging talk

• Help toddlers to talk about events by asking questions, such as 'What was on top of your birthday cake?' You could make a scrapbook about a special event, so you can revisit it again and again.

• Make up a bedtime story together about your toddler's day. It helps if you start off and let them join in as you go along. Ask questions such as 'Where did we go today? Who did we see? What did we do?'

Toddlers love to help out around the house and this can be an ideal opportunity to talk about everyday life. Let them do simple tasks, such as sweeping, dusting or tidying away toys, and talk to them about what they're doing and why. Remember to give them lots of praise, even if you have to do the job again yourself later on!

Looking at photos together is a great way to help toddlers learn the names of friends and family. If they can't yet say the names themselves, see if they can point to people as you name them. With older toddlers, you can use photos to talk about past events, such as birthdays or holidays.

Let's pretend

Between the ages of one and two, toddlers learn enough about how the world works to start imagining things and pretending. Pretend play encourages children to try out new ways of expressing themselves. Young toddlers may enjoy pretend tea parties or putting their teddy bear to bed, while older toddlers might be ready for more complicated role-play, dressing up as doctors, firefighters or fairies. It's helpful if you join in, but try not to take over.

Provide items for dressing up, such as old hats, bags, gloves, shawls and jewellery. These are easier for toddlers to manage than clothes.

You could make a puppet from an old sock by sticking on fabric eyes, ears and tongue. Or draw a face on a wooden spoon and stick on some fabric for a dress and wool for hair.

Encourage role-play by providing simple play materials. An old box can become anything from a fire engine to a fairytale castle.

Rhymes and songs

Singing songs and nursery rhymes together is a fun way to help toddlers learn new words and phrases. It also gives them an awareness of rhyme, which is an important pre-reading skill. Toddlers will often want to sing the same song over and over again, but try to be patient as repetition is really useful for language learning. Using tapes or CDs of children's songs will give you a break for a while and can help pass the time on long car journeys.

Toddlers can join in with action rhymes long before they know all the words.

Talking to others

Whenever you can, try to give toddlers opportunities to talk to other children and adults. Encourage family members and friends to talk to your toddler, and let them talk back. You may need to 'translate' if their language isn't clear, but try not to answer for them.

Toddler groups are a great way for small children to start making friends of their own age.

Useful tip

Local libraries often run rhyme sessions for toddlers that you can join free of charge.

Talking and television

Television can be useful for making links with books and getting toddlers interested in stories, but it will only help their language learning if you use it as a starting point for conversations. Toddlers should only watch programmes designed for their age group and shouldn't watch too much – they'll benefit much more from playing and talking.

It's best to watch television with your toddler, so you can talk about anything that catches their attention.

Beginning with books

The most important thing you can do to help your child become a reader is to enjoy books together – and it's never too early to start. Babies can have fun with books long before they know any words, and they'll also be picking up skills they will need later when they begin learning to read.

Children who enjoy books are more likely to become good readers than those who don't, and the best way to give them a love of books is by reading to them from a very young age. Even small babies love listening to the sound of your voice as you share books cuddled up together, and they soon come to associate reading with this positive feeling of warmth and security.

By looking at books, children become familiar with how books and stories work. As babies, they learn which way up to hold a book and how to turn the pages. Later on, they get to know that stories have a beginning, a middle and an end, and often follow a predictable pattern. They also become familiar with storybook language, which is more formal than everyday speech. These are all vital skills that will help a child learn to read when the time comes.

Note

On the next few pages, 'babies' refers to children under 12 months.

Research has shown that babies and toddlers who are read to regularly tend to do better at reading when they start school.

Why read to babies and toddlers?

- Babies and toddlers who are read to a lot often have longer attention spans.
- Reading to toddlers helps them to learn new words and become better talkers.
- Books can help in tackling issues such as potty training or a new baby.
- Sharing storybooks together helps toddlers to recognize and talk about their feelings.

Choosing books

There are so many children's books around that choosing the right ones can seem a daunting task. Remember that babies explore by touching, pulling, shaking and chewing, so books need to be tough. For babies under six months, cloth books or plastic bath books are best. Board books are ideal for older babies and toddlers, as the pages won't tear and are thick enough for them to be able to turn. Books with noises, textures, tabs, flaps to lift or holes to peep through are great for getting babies and toddlers involved.

- Newborn babies like to look at pictures of faces, as well as bold patterns with sharp outlines in contrasting colours, such as black and white.
- A book of children's poems or nursery rhymes is a must. The regular rhythms of rhymes and poetry are soothing and can help to get babies to sleep.

Try some very simple information books. Animals, farms and vehicles are popular topics.

Tabs help turn pages.

First word books are ideal for babies and toddlers who are just starting to talk.

Books with different textures are fun to explore and help to develop sensory awareness.

red

apple

door

cherries

gloves

car

fire engine

tomato

ketchup

strawberry

Books about concepts such as size, colours, numbers and counting are a good choice for toddlers.

Stories and rhymes

Experts recommend reading to babies right from birth as it helps to develop their language and concentration. Simple poems and nursery rhymes can act as 'stories' for even the tiniest of babies. For toddlers, try adding in folk tales, fairy tales and animal stories. These need to be very simple, with lots of bright, clear pictures. Look out for stories that repeat catchy, rhythmical phrases over and over again, as these give babies and toddlers something to listen out for and help them to see language as fun.

- Stories about everyday routines or familiar experiences are great because you can easily link them to a child's own experiences.
- Remember that some fairy tales can be quite frightening. Stop reading if a child seems scared or disturbed.

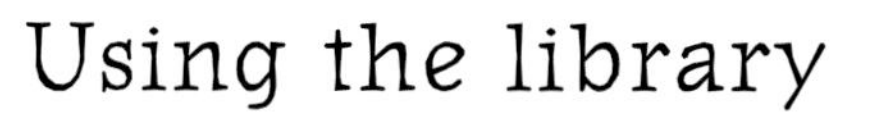

Using the library

Your local library is a great place to start looking for books. The children's librarian can help if you're not sure which books to choose, and by trying out different titles you'll soon find out which ones your child likes. Joining the library is free and you can enrol babies as members from birth. Aim to take toddlers regularly and let them choose their own books as soon as they're able to.

By hearing the librarian read, you can pick up some hints for reading aloud.

Libraries often run story sessions for toddlers. These are great for encouraging an interest in books.

Books for keeps

If you want to buy books, a book shop with a specialist children's section will have the widest choice, but you can pick up secondhand books at jumble sales, charity shops and fairs at toddler groups, preschools and infant schools. It's worth checking out book clubs and internet retailers, which often sell books at discount prices. Encourage family members to buy books as gifts, or try swapping with friends – but don't give away books your child really likes.

It's important to find a special place for children to keep their books. It should be somewhere they can reach easily, so a low shelf is ideal. You could use a sturdy box or basket, but make sure that crawling babies can reach inside.

A shallow cardboard box, covered in giftwrap, makes a good book box for crawling babies.

Looking at books

Books will get sucked and chewed, so check them often and wipe them clean.

Try to encourage babies to look at books on their own from an early age, even if they only play with them at first. It's a good idea to put a favourite book in your bag every time you go out, so children always have something to look at. This sends the message that books are an essential part of life right from the start. Bear in mind that children are much more likely to look at books themselves if they see you reading for pleasure yourself.

Reading together

Babies have a very short attention span, so it's best to look at books little and often. Start with short sessions of just a few minutes at a time, spread at intervals throughout the day. As their concentration improves, you can gradually lengthen the time you spend reading together.

From about 12 months, try to set up regular reading times, maybe first thing in the morning, after lunch, before a nap or at bedtime. Bedtime stories often become an important part of a child's routine and can be continued long after children are able to read for themselves.

Studies show that women tend to read to children more than men, but it's very important – particularly for boys – that dads, or other male relatives, read to children as often as they can.

Tips for reading together

- Don't drag children away from something they're enjoying to look at books.
- Switch off any distracting background noise, such as the television or radio.
- Sit somewhere comfortable and hold your baby in your lap. Let toddlers snuggle up to you.
- If your child isn't interested, stop and try again later.

Remember to have fun together. The more children enjoy books, the more they will want to look at them.

Reading to babies

As you read, look at each page in turn and give your baby time to look at the pictures. Wait for them to coo or point at things that interest them, and respond when they do. Point to the pictures on the page, say the names of objects and describe what you can see. It's good to ask lots of questions, such as 'Where's the cat? Can you see its tail?', even though you'll have to answer the questions yourself.

Useful tip

You can find out more about books for babies and toddlers by going to **www.usborne-quicklinks.com** and typing in 'babies and books'.

Reading to toddlers

Before reading a book to your toddler, try to find time to read it yourself first. Stories are easier to read aloud if you're already familiar with them, and you can spot things in advance that your toddler might find puzzling or disturbing.

Let babies and toddlers touch or hold a book and turn the pages. When they lose interest, put the book away.

Encourage toddlers to choose which book they want to read, and let them hold the book and turn the pages. The first time you read a book, they may just want to look through it, so don't worry if you have to miss out bits of the story. The main thing is to let them enjoy exploring the book – you can read the whole story another time.

Expect toddlers to interrupt, and be ready to respond if they make a comment or ask a question.

Reading to toddlers

- Before you start reading, look at the front of the book and say the title.
- Read slowly enough to let the story sink in and allow time to look at the pictures.
- Use lots of expression and have fun with sound effects, such as 'woof' for a dog.
- Follow the words with your finger, so children realize you're reading the print.
- Encourage toddlers to join in with rhyming and repeated text, as they get to know it.

Talking and playing

Talking about a book helps to get toddlers involved and is an excellent way of developing their language skills at the same time. As you read, talk about the pictures and point out things your toddler might have missed. Ask young toddlers to point to things in a picture as you name them. As their language develops, see if they can name things as you point to them. You could also ask simple questions about how the characters in a story might feel.

Try to link the text and pictures to a toddler's own experiences. For example, point out a red ball and ask what colour their ball is.

When you're out, make links back to stories you've read. If you see a friend's dog, talk about one you've met in a book.

You could use simple props, such as toy animals, vehicles or home-made puppets (see right and on page 12), to help tell a favourite story. This can really bring the story to life, and encourages toddlers to use it as a basis for pretend play.

Again! Again!

Toddlers love to hear their favourite stories over and over again, so be prepared to read the same book many, many times. This constant repetition gives toddlers confidence and is really important for their language learning – they need to hear a word or phrase many times before they can use it themselves. They also need to learn that the language of a story stays the same no matter how often you read it. Above all, they need to have fun!

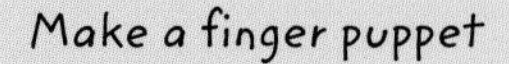

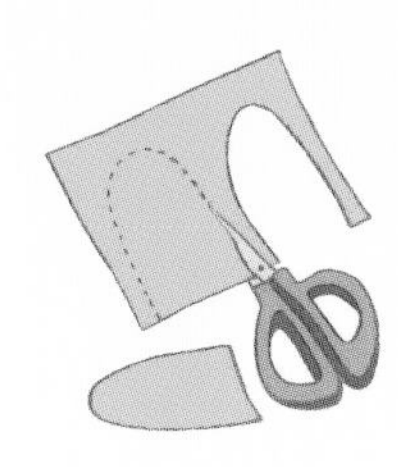

1. Cut out two finger-length shapes like this from card or paper.

2. Glue the edges of the two shapes together leaving the bottom open.

3. Cut out a shape for the head. Draw in a face and stick it on. Stick on a tail.

4. You can adapt this basic shape to make lots of different characters.

Making marks

When babies play with spilt food and drink, using their palms and fingers to create patterns, they aren't just making a mess – they're making marks. This is the first step on a child's journey to writing.

From about 12 months, you can encourage toddlers' mark-making by giving them different surfaces to explore. Before you start, make sure you are both wearing aprons or old clothes, and spread a plastic sheet or some newspaper over the floor and table. You'll find more ideas to try on the Usborne Quicklinks Website (see page 84).

Safety point

Make sure all mark-making materials are non-toxic and washable.

Put some sand in a big plastic bowl, dampen it with water and let toddlers make marks in it. Use play sand, not builder's sand, as it won't stain.

Squeeze some thick paint onto a tray. Let toddlers move it around with their fingers and make handprints on paper.

Splodges and scribbles

At around 18 months, start introducing chunky crayons or thick marker pens and lots of scrap paper for scribbling. At this age, toddlers may still find holding a paintbrush tricky, but they can paint just as well with pieces of sponge, cardboard or scrunched-up fabric – or with their fingers. As they scribble and paint, they gradually learn to control the muscles in their hands and start to develop the hand-eye co-ordination they will need for writing.

It's important to value toddlers' efforts, so be enthusiastic about whatever they show you. Stick their pictures on the walls of the kitchen or bedroom and remember to change the display regularly.

- Cut a potato in half, brush the flat surface with paint and show toddlers how to make prints on paper.

- Chalks are fun for scribbling on a pavement or patio. Rain will wash the scribbles off.

- Let toddlers 'paint' on a fence or wall using a bucket of water and a large brush or roller.

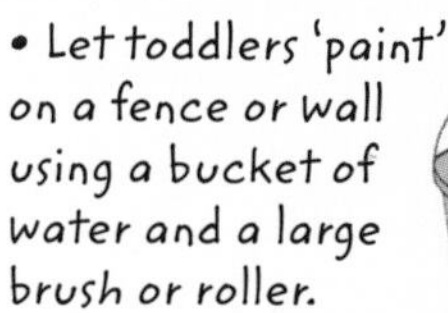

Preschoolers

The year or two before children start school is crucial in preparing them for learning to read and write. In this section, you'll find lots of ideas to help them develop the skills they will need. It's vital, too, that children develop a positive attitude to reading and writing, so when choosing activities always be guided by what your child enjoys.

Key skills at a glance

Adding new words to their spoken vocabulary and talking in longer sentences

Listening carefully and understanding what is said to them

Enjoying books and becoming familiar with a range of stories and rhymes

Recognizing print and knowing what it's for

Picking out sounds in spoken words

Knowing some of the letters of the alphabet and how to form them

Using a pencil with some control

Keep talking

- Show how to take turns in conversations by listening carefully and then responding.
- Allow children time to speak and don't rush them or finish their sentences for them.
- Try to be patient with their endless questions and answer at a level they will understand.
- Give children plenty of opportunities to talk to other children of the same age.

It's vital for children to develop good language skills before they start school – almost everything they will be expected to learn depends on their ability to understand and use language. It sounds simple, but the best way you can help is to spend time talking and listening to your child.

Although children may be able to talk fairly well by the age of three, their language is still developing. For the next couple of years, they go on learning words and grammar at an amazing speed. Most add about 50 to 70 new words to their vocabulary every week, and their sentences get longer and more complex. By the time they're five, their grammar knowledge will be much the same as an adult's.

Tips for talking

Activities such as cooking and baking together provide great opportunities for conversations.

Young children learn language best through conversations with other people. The key is to listen to what they have to say and continue the conversation from there. If your child says 'I did painting at nursery', you could reply 'You did painting? That sounds fun! What did you paint?' This reassures them that what they've said was correct and encourages them to go on talking. Don't discourage children by criticizing their mistakes or trying to stop them using baby language. If they get a word wrong, just repeat their sentence back to them correctly and expand on what they've said. So if your child says 'Granny buyed me a cookie', you could reply 'She bought you a cookie? You *are* lucky! Did it taste nice?'

Building language

Everything you and your child do together can be an opportunity to talk. Ask lots of open-ended questions, for example 'What did you play with at nursery today?' or 'What do you think will happen if you leave the bath tap on?' Follow the child's lead whenever you can, and encourage them to express opinions and make decisions, such as which toy to take on a day out.

Before learning to read, children need to have a good basic vocabulary. They can only understand words they see in print if they've already come across them in speech. You can introduce new words naturally by playing games, making things, going on outings or reading books together.

Things to talk about

- Involve children in planning the day ahead and talk about what clothes to wear.
- Do jigsaw puzzles together and think out loud as you work out which pieces fit where.
- Provide old clothes for dressing up and join in with your child's pretend play.
- Show children photos of a family outing and see if they can retell the day's events.

If you visit a zoo or wildlife park, you can name and describe the animals, and ask children what they think about them.

Language games

The games shown below will encourage children to search for the words they need to describe things. The first two can be played anywhere, so are handy for passing the time while travelling or waiting at the doctor's. You'll find some more ideas on the Usborne Quicklinks Website (see page 84).

- Pretend to be an animal or a child's favourite toy. Can children work out what (or who) you are by asking simple 'yes' or 'no' questions, such as 'Can you fly?' or 'Do you have a tail?'
- Choose two objects, such as an apple and a ball, a sock and a shoe, or a cat and a dog. Together, try to find two things the same and two things that are different about each pair of objects.
- Make a 'feely box'. Put some familiar objects in a box with two hand-holes cut in the side. Children put their hands in and try to describe what they feel before guessing what it is.

Learning to listen

Get children to close their eyes and keep very still, then see how many different sounds they can hear. You can play this inside or out.

Ask children to close their eyes and guess what you're doing, e.g. closing a door, blowing your nose, sharpening a pencil, bouncing a ball.

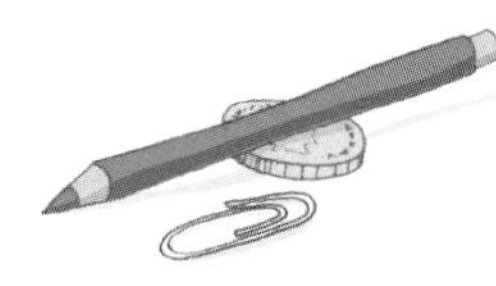

Choose three objects (e.g. a coin, a paperclip, a pencil) and drop them into a box or tin. Your child has to guess which item is being dropped.

Listening skills play an important part in communication and learning, and are essential for learning to read. Yet we live in such a noisy world that many children get used to shutting out background sounds and only half-listening. There are lots of ways you can encourage young children to listen properly, but don't expect miracles. It may take time and lots of practice.

To learn how to read, children must be able to hear that words are made up of different sounds. First, they need to be able to focus their attention on listening and become aware of as many different sounds as possible. On the left, you'll find some suggestions for activities that will help, and there are links to online listening games on the Usborne Quicklinks Website (see page 84). Young children often find it difficult to concentrate on listening for very long, so if they get restless, stop and try something else.

Listening to stories, read by you or on CD, will also help extend your child's attention span.

1. Try clapping out the number of syllables in your child's name. For example, as you say 'Ka-tie' you would clap twice.

2. Do this for other family members, e.g. 'Da-ddy,' then get your child to clap as they name other people they know.

Rhyme and rhythm

A familiarity with rhyme and the rhythm of language helps children become aware of the sounds that make up different words. Children love rhymes, and sharing nursery rhymes, poems and rhyming stories together is a great way to help them focus on the sounds in words. Encourage children to join in and make it fun by clapping along or adding movement and actions in time to the rhythm.

Rhyming games

Games, like those in the panel on the right, are a fun way to teach children about rhyme and encourage their curiosity about the sound of language. Most children enjoy playing around with rhyme once they get the hang of it, but some find it very difficult. If you get a blank response, just leave it for a while and try again in a few weeks.

Rhyming games

- Say a list of words, all but one of which rhyme, e.g. cat, sat, shine, mat. See if your child can spot the odd one out.
- Play a rhyming version of 'I spy,' giving clues if needed, e.g. 'I spy with my little eye something that rhymes with "hat". It says "meow".'
- Choose a one-syllable word, such as 'pig,' and take turns to think of words that rhyme with it. Nonsense words are fine!

A sound memory

The ability to remember exactly what you've heard is called auditory memory and it's important for all school-based learning, including literacy skills. To become readers, children need to remember the sounds that the letters of the alphabet represent, as well as the meanings of words they hear and the sense of what they've just read. Here are some ways to help develop a child's auditory memory:

- Play 'On my magic island I would have...' or 'I went to the shops and bought...', taking it in turns to add something to the list, each time repeating all the items already listed.
- Ask children to listen hard, remember what you've said and then do it. Start with just one instruction, e.g. 'Find a book.' Build up to two, three and then four instructions.

See if your child can copy simple rhythms tapped out on a toy drum or on a saucepan with a spoon or pencil.

Singing along with rhyming songs and action rhymes helps to improve children's memory and develops their awareness of rhyme and rhythm.

Matching games

- Make two identical sets of cards with a simple shape drawn on each card. Get children to match the shapes.
- Make it harder by adding in cards with the same shapes in different colours (e.g. two blue and two red squares).
- Use the cards to play a memory game, where you turn over two cards at a time to find matching pairs.
- Put all the shapes in a bag, draw one out and go on a shape hunt to find something else which is that shape.

Plastic or wooden beads are good for sorting. Small beads are dangerous for young children, but you can buy large ones from toy shops.

Learning to look

To learn to read, children need to be able to look closely at the shapes of letters and spot small differences between them. They also have to be able to remember what each letter looks like. Here you'll find lots of ideas to help young children develop good observation skills and improve their visual memory.

Matching

Being able to spot two things that look the same is an important skill for children to learn. When you're sorting clean laundry, try getting them to help you match up the socks. Or collect some of the family's shoes together and make a game of sorting them into pairs.

On some paper, draw around different objects, e.g. a coin, pencil, rubber, scissors, cookie cutters, and see if children can match the objects to the outline.

Simple sticker books, where children have to match coloured stickers with line drawings, are a fun way to practise matching. Or try snap cards and lotto games.

Sorting

Simple household jobs can provide lots of opportunities for sorting activities. Children could sort the forks, spoons and knives (but not sharp knives) before you put them away. Or let them help you sort the laundry into different piles. You could collect buttons from old clothes to sort into groups or encourage children to sort their building blocks into different shapes, sizes and colours.

Finding and spotting

Pictures in books are really useful for developing children's observation skills. Pick a busy scene with lots of detail and ask children to find objects in the picture. For example, see if they can spot a yellow duck or find a boy with an ice cream. Simple jigsaw puzzles and 'Spot the difference' pictures are also great for getting children to look at details.

1. To make your own 'Spot the difference' pictures, create a scene using items from a doll's house or a toy farm or garage.

2. Take a picture of the scene with a digital camera. Remove or replace some items, and take another picture.

3. Print out the two pictures, as large as possible, and see if children can find the differences between them.

1. To play a memory version of 'Spot the difference', put a selection of familiar objects on a tray.

2. Ask your child to look closely at the objects for a few moments.

3. Without your child seeing, take one object away, then ask if they can spot which one is missing.

Nature walks are great for encouraging children to look closely at things.

Your child could try following an ant or looking at bugs through a magnifying glass.

Take children to a wood or park and collect lots of different leaves. At home, ask them to sort the leaves into groups and make a collage.

Seeing sequences

You can use toy building blocks to help children recognize sequences. First, create a repeating pattern of blocks, such as red, blue, red, blue, and so on, then see if children can copy it. You can make this activity more difficult by using more colours or more complicated patterns. Once children get the idea, see if they can make a pattern for you to copy.

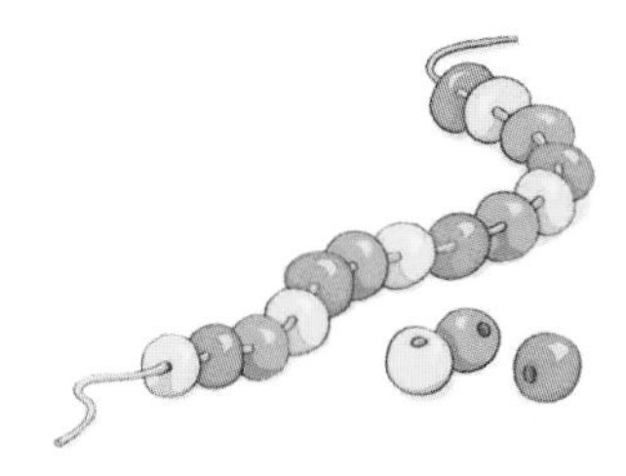

You could thread large beads in a repeating pattern and ask your child to copy it.

Books for preschoolers

- Stories that stimulate your child's imagination, such as fairy tales, legends and stories with animal characters.

- Stories about everyday life that children can relate to, with main characters their own age or slightly older.

- Poems, nursery rhymes and rhyming stories with repetitive refrains that children can remember.

- Longer storybooks divided into short chapters that children can listen to over several sessions.

Back to books

Reading aloud to young children is the most important thing you can do to prepare them for learning to read. It broadens their vocabulary, helps them to listen and concentrate better, introduces them to the idea of print and builds their knowledge of the world around them. Most of all, it shows them that reading is fun and encourages them to want to learn to read for themselves.

Choosing books

The aim in choosing books is to find ones a child will really enjoy. A good starting point is to look for books that reflect your child's interests or tie in with their experiences. For example, before or after a trip to the beach, you might choose a story set at the seaside and an information book about seashore animals.

When choosing storybooks, look for simple, fun plots and vivid illustrations with lots of detail. Try to expose children to as wide a variety of books as you can, both fiction and non-fiction, but don't worry if your child prefers one type of book to another. There are some suggestions below and in the panel on the left.

Alphabet books or flashcards, and books about numbers, counting, colours or shapes are ideal for preschoolers.

Look for information books with lots of colourful pictures, interesting facts and simple explanations.

Using the library

Borrowing books from the library is the best way to give children lots of variety. Take children often and help them to choose their own books. If you're unsure, you can always ask the librarian for advice about books to suit your child's needs and interests. Let children take their books to the desk to be stamped and teach them to treat the books carefully so that other children can enjoy them too.

Useful tip

Ask about preschool activities at your library. Many libraries run free rhyme and story sessions, puppet shows or craft activities.

Books for keeps

As well as having access to library books, it's important that children have some books of their own. Children who own books learn to love them and tend to become better readers. On page 16, you'll find some hints for buying books cheaply.

It's important too to keep children's books somewhere they can easily reach them, such as a low shelf or bookcase. Having a special place for books shows children that books are important.

Placing a beanbag or a comfortable chair next to a bookshelf makes a cosy book corner.

Reading routine

Experts recommend that parents read to their children every day. If you read at the same time each day, such as bedtime, it will quickly become a habit – and one that children look forward to. They love the physical closeness and the individual attention you give them as you read, and this affects the way they feel about books.

Remember that reading shouldn't be confined to bedtime. As far as possible, read to children whenever they ask you and carry a book with you wherever you go, so you always have something to keep them entertained.

Setting the scene

- Choose a comfortable place to read aloud and let children snuggle up to you.
- Turn off the television or radio, so children can listen without any distractions.
- Don't insist on reading if children aren't in the mood – it could turn them off books.
- Remember that dads, or other male relatives, should read to children too – especially boys.

Reading aloud

Tips for reading aloud

- Follow the words with your finger as you read. This shows a child that the print tells the story and that it's read from top to bottom and left to right.
- As a story becomes familiar, encourage children to join in with rhyming or repeated text by leaving out key words and letting the child supply them.

It's easier to read a story in a lively, expressive way if you're already familiar with it, so try to find time to read a new book yourself first. This also gives you the chance to spot any words or details that might need explaining. Before you start, look at the cover together, point out the title and the author's name, and ask children what they think the book might be about. Predicting how stories might turn out is a valuable skill that helps children to become good readers.

As you're reading, stop every so often to make a comment on the text or pictures, or to ask a question. The illustrations are an important part of a picture book, so give children plenty of time to look at them, and talk together about what you see. The panel on the left shows the kinds of questions you might ask. Remember the aim is to involve children and help them to enjoy books – you're not testing them. Keep it light and have fun!

Talking about books

- What's happening in this picture?
- I wonder why the prince did that?
- How do you think he felt?
- What do you think will happen next?
- Which bit of the story did you like best?
- Is it like any other stories we've read?

As well as talking about books, make sure children have lots of opportunities just to enjoy listening quietly as you read, so they can really focus on the story and learn to concentrate. Reading a longer story over several sessions is a good way to develop your child's memory and attention skills.

It helps if you relate what you read to your child's experiences, for example linking a plane in a story to one you just saw in the sky.

Pretend reading

Young children who have been read to a lot often pretend to read books by themselves or to dolls and soft toys. As they turn the pages, they may point to the text and make up their own words to go with the pictures – or even re-tell the whole story from memory. Here are some ways to encourage this important phase:

If young children are pretending to read, it shows that they see books as fun.

- When you read together, see if children can re-tell parts of the story themselves by looking at the pictures.
- Ask a child to tell you the story of one of their books while you're doing jobs around the house.
- Look at a picture book without words and encourage your child to make up a story based on the pictures.
- Show children that you enjoy reading. Let them see you reading books, newspapers or magazines.

Book and story activities

Some of these activities are designed just to encourage a child's enjoyment of books. Others practise useful pre-reading skills, such as understanding that stories are made up of a sequence of events in a particular order.

- Act out a favourite story together using props such as dressing-up clothes, hats, bags or toys. You won't need many props as young children have such vivid imaginations.
- Make a story sack to introduce a new book. This is a cloth bag containing a picture book, some props to help tell or act out the the story and a non-fiction book on a similar theme.
- Cut up a comic strip or a simple picture sequence (there are some to print out on the Usborne Quicklinks Website). Get children to talk about the pictures and put them in order.
- Tell stories together. On holiday, help children to tell the story of their holiday, adding in more each day. You could also tell them about things that happened to you as a child.

Make a story sequence

1. Choose some photos of a special event, such as a birthday or a day out. Talk about the photos together and see if children can put them in the right order.

2. Stick the photos into a scrapbook and get children to tell you what to write next to each photo. When you look at the book together, let them re-tell the day's events.

If you eat out, show children the menu and read out the things they might like.

A world of print

Knowing about print – what it looks like and what it's for – is called print awareness. Studies show that children who have a good awareness of print before they start school are at a big advantage when they begin learning to read.

To develop print awareness, children have to learn that print is different from pictures and that there's a link between the words an adult reads out loud and the squiggly lines on the page of a book. They need to know that print is read from top to bottom and from left to right, and that it's made up of separate words.

You can help by reading to children regularly and by showing them the many different ways that print is used in everyday life. Books are vitally important, but try reading all kinds of other things as well. We're surrounded by print, so the opportunities are endless.

'Spot the sign' game

1. Print out some pictures of road signs. There are some on the Usborne Quicklinks Website (see page 84).

2. Stick the pictures onto a piece of card.

3. When you go out, see if children can spot the signs shown on the card.

Out and about

When you go out, point out posters, traffic signs and signs for familiar places, such as the park or supermarket, or the name of the road or town where you live. You could turn it into a game, for example by seeing how many 'STOP' signs you can spot together as you walk or drive along.

When you visit the swimming pool, point out and explain the list of pool rules.

At home

Any time you read anything, for example when you follow a recipe, check a bus timetable or look up a telephone number, talk about what you're doing and tell children what the print says. Look at greetings cards, invitations and postcards together and read them out loud. You can help children to include reading in their pretend play by giving them a selection of printed materials to play with.

Print awareness activities

- Ask your family to write letters or emails to your child. Let the child dictate a reply and read it back to them before you send it.

- Make some menu cards with words and pictures for playing restaurants. Give the 'waiter' or 'waitress' a pad and pencil to scribble the order on.

Keep magazine recipes next to the play dough to help with pretend cooking.

Leave an old phone book by the play phone, so children can 'look up' numbers.

Recognizing words

Even before they learn to read, children may start to recognize the shapes of words that they see often. Most young children are interested in seeing their name written down and this is often the first word they learn to read. It's important not to pressurize children into trying to recognize words – keep it fun and don't push it if they're not interested. Here are a few ideas to try:

- Show children their name in print and write out name labels that they can stick on their possessions.

- Point out words that you see often, such as the name of their favourite drink, snack or breakfast cereal.

- Tape labels to drawers and cupboards showing what's inside, e.g. 'knives, forks, spoons' on the cutlery drawer.

- Lotto games which have pictures and simple words are a fun way for children to see words in print.

Useful tip

Print labels clearly, using a capital letter at the start of a child's name. All other letters should be lower-case.

Playing with sounds

As you read stories or poems with alliteration, ask children to clap when they hear a word starting with that sound.

To learn to read, children need to know the sounds that the letters of the alphabet make and be able to link those sounds with the shapes of the written letters. The first step towards learning letters is becoming aware of the different sounds that make up words.

Children find it easiest to pick out sounds at the start of words, so it's best to focus on these first. Read stories, poems and rhymes with lots of alliteration (words starting with the same sound) and ask children to listen out for words that start with a particular sound. Try using alliteration in everyday conversations, for example asking children if they'd like some 'sizzling sausages' or some 'crunchy carrots', and have fun saying tongue twisters together. There's a list of tongue twisters on the Usborne Quicklinks Website (see page 84).

Get children to look in a mirror as they say different sounds, so they can see how their lips and tongue move.

Noticing sounds in words

- Make up tongue twisters based around your child's name, e.g. 'Clever Katie caught a kicking cat.'
- Point out things that start with the same sound as your child's name and say the sound on its own.
- When you're talking about sounds, try not to add an 'uh' to the sound. Say 'sss' not 'suh' and 'mmm' not 'muh.'

Games are a fun way to focus on the sounds in words, but it's important that children get a feeling of success from playing with sounds. Give them lots of encouragement and make sure any games aren't too difficult for them. If a child is struggling, stop and try again in a few weeks.

Sound games

To begin with, try some matching games where children have to find a picture or object beginning with a particular sound. Many four-year-olds will struggle if they have too many pictures to choose from, so start with just three or four and build up from there.

Spread out some picture cards on the floor and ask your child to jump on something beginning with 'rrr'. Continue with different sounds.

Sound-matching games

To play these games, you need picture cards of familiar objects. Use flashcards, cards from a lotto game, or stick pictures from a catalogue onto pieces of card.

1. Start with just two different sounds. See if children can help you sort the cards into two piles, e.g. '"Sofa", does that start with "sss" or "mmm"?'

2. Set out four cards, all but one beginning with the same sound. See if your child can spot the odd one out. Reinforce by saying 'Yes! "Apple" starts with "ah".'

3. Sort the cards so there are matching pairs starting with the same sound. Mix them up, spread them out face up and take it in turns to find the pairs.

Once children are confident at matching initial sounds to pictures or objects, you can try games where they have to think up different words beginning with the same sound.

When you go for a walk, choose a particular sound and see how many things you can spot together starting with that sound.

- Play 'I spy with my little eye something beginning with...' (remember to use the sound, not the letter). Take turns choosing objects for each other to guess.

- Play 'I'm going to the seaside and I'm taking a sss...' Take turns to add words, such as 'spade' or 'sausage'. Try other destinations, such as 'the Moon' or 'the playground'.

- Look at a scene from a book together and see how many things you can find beginning with the same sound.

Learning letters

Useful tip
Teach children lower-case (small) letters, but use a capital for the first letter of their name.

Once children have had lots of practice at picking out the sounds in words, you can gradually introduce them to the written letters that stand for some of these sounds. It's important not to push young children into learning letters too soon, so keep it fun, make learning a game and stop if your child is struggling or isn't interested.

Letters aren't usually taught in alphabetical order, but by how commonly they're used in words. Take it slowly and introduce one letter at a time. It's a good idea to start with the letters in your child's name, then move on to 's', 'a', 't', 'p', 'i' and 'n', perhaps followed by 'm', 'd', 'g', 'o', 'c' and 'e'. There's no need to teach children all the letters of the alphabet before they start school.

- Try to connect letters with things that are important to your child. Most children are fascinated by the letters in their own name.
- Studies show that children who know the shapes and sounds of some of the letters before they start school find it easier to learn to read.

When you introduce each new letter, remember to link the written letter with the sound it makes. Try to pronounce the sounds as clearly as you can. The Usborne Quicklinks Website has an online pronunciation guide to help you say the letter sounds correctly (see page 84).

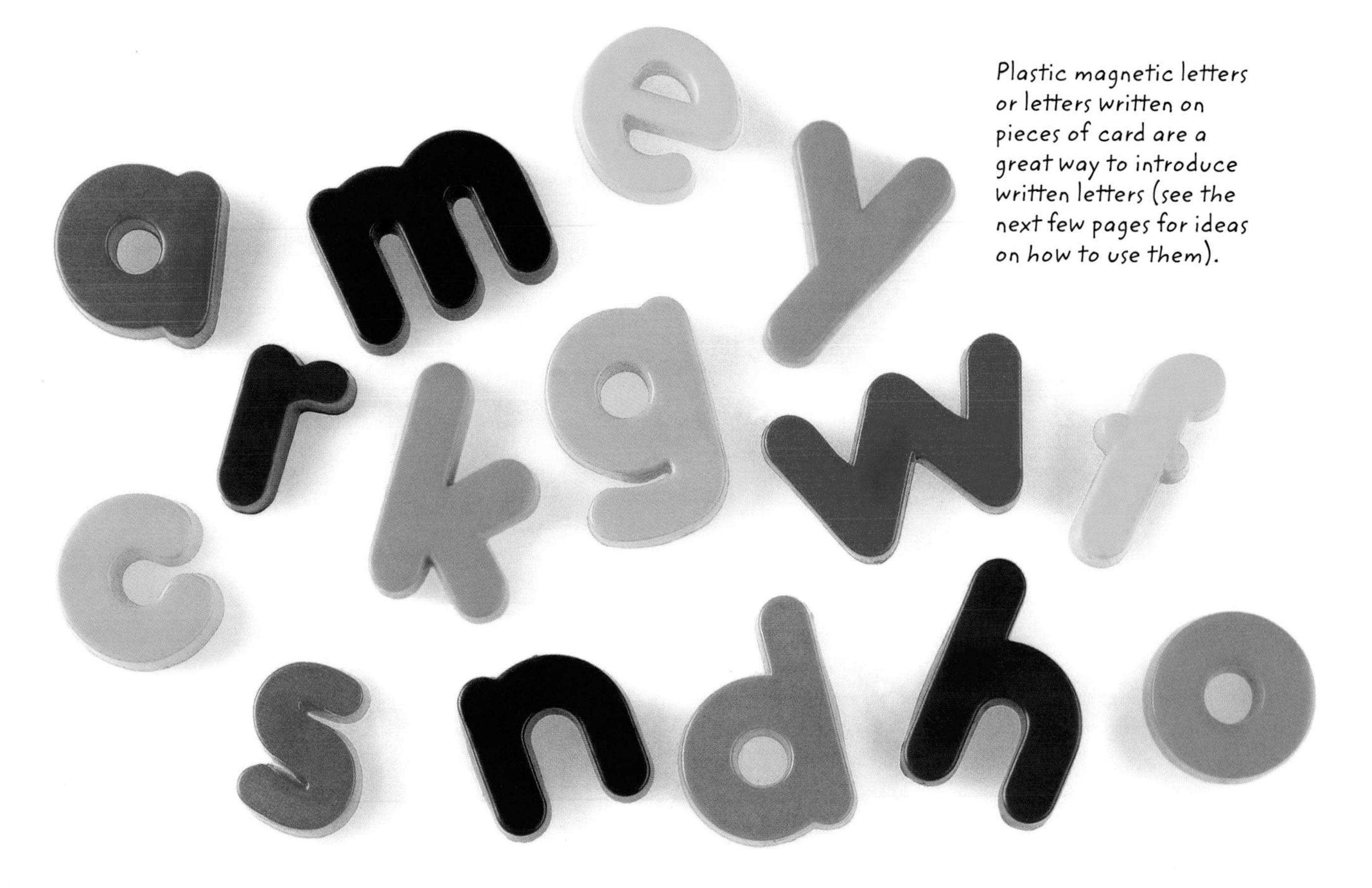

Plastic magnetic letters or letters written on pieces of card are a great way to introduce written letters (see the next few pages for ideas on how to use them).

Letter by letter

A fun way to introduce new letters is to use a letter-sound box. First, collect some objects together that begin with the same letter and sound, and put them in a cardboard box. Take each object out very slowly and see if your child can guess what it is. Emphasize the initial sound of the object as you pull it out, for example saying 'It's a d-d-d-d-doll!' Set all the objects on the table, then put a letter 'd' next to them and say, 'This letter makes a "d" sound – "d" for "doll", "duck" and "dog". Can you think of some other things beginning with "d"?'

Use a glue stick or glue pen to write a particular letter shape on paper, then let children shake on glitter and watch the letter appear.

It's best to do lots of activities with each new letter before moving on to the next one. Here are a few ideas to try (see also pages 43 and 44 for writing activities):

Ask children to hunt around the house for objects starting with a particular letter sound, then display all the objects with the letter.

Play 'Spot the letter' in books and on food packets, road signs and posters. Let children circle letters they find in magazines and newspapers.

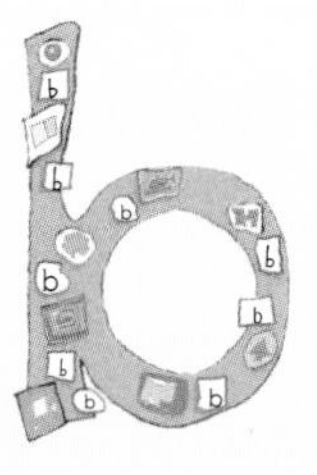

Make a letter collage together, using cut-out letters from magazines and pictures of objects starting with that letter sound.

Make a letter scrapbook

1. Look through magazines and old catalogues together and have fun cutting out pictures of things starting with a chosen letter sound.

2. Write the letter at the top of a scrapbook page and let children stick in the pictures. Add to the scrapbook as you introduce new letters.

Playing with letters

It's important to keep going back over letters children have already learned, so they don't forget them. Books, games and toys are great for helping children to revise letters in different ways, so they don't get bored. Vary the activities often, adding in new letters as children learn them, and remember to keep emphasizing the letter sounds.

Plastic magnetic letters are especially useful. Put some on the refrigerator or on any safe metal surface, such as a baking tray, and let children move them around as they say the letter sounds. Show them their name, then mix up the letters and see if they can put them back in the right order. Try making a simple word like 'cat', then changing the first letter to make other words, such as 'sat' or 'mat', but don't expect children to spell words themselves yet.

Letter-sound activities

- Put a few of the letters your child knows into a bag. Choose a category, such as animals, food or toys. Pick a letter and take turns to think of words in that category starting with that letter.

- Set out a few of the letters your child knows, then say a sound and see if the child can pick out the letter that makes that sound.

- Look out for DVDs that link letter sounds and shapes. Or you could play letter-sound games together online. You'll find links to useful websites on the Usborne Quicklinks Website (see page 84).

Make some letter-shaped biscuits using alphabet cookie cutters or by forming letters from thin rolls of dough.

If children can name five things starting with 'sss', for example, they get to eat the 's'-shaped biscuit.

Make or buy a lotto board with some letters on it, plus picture cards showing objects starting with those letters. Children have to turn over the cards and match them to the initial letters on the board.

Alphabet activities

Once children are familiar with a few letter sounds, you can introduce the idea that letters also have a name – so the letter that makes a 'sss' sound is called 's'. Alphabet books are a great way of doing this. Look at the book together and find a letter your child knows. Encourage the child to say the letter sound, tell them what the letter is called and show them how to trace over the letter shape with their finger (see page 92 for the correct way to form the letters). Let children look at alphabet books on their own, too, and answer any questions they ask.

Children don't need to be able to recite the whole alphabet before they start school, but it's helpful for them to see that the letters are always written down in the same order. Some alphabet books have games and songs that you can enjoy together, but don't push children into learning alphabetical order before they're ready.

Let children play with letters in as many different ways as possible. Being able to touch and feel the letters helps a child to remember them.

It's a good idea to put up an alphabet frieze in your child's room at a height they can reach. You could even make one together using pictures from magazines.

Use a frieze to practise the letters. Say one sound at a time and see if your child can point to the right letter. Try getting them to say letter sounds for you to find.

Make a book

1. Make a simple book together using some stiff paper, a hole punch and some ribbon to tie it together.

2. Let your child think of a topic, such as a favourite toy or a day out. Write the title and their name on the front.

3. Encourage your child to tell you what to write and let them draw or stick in pictures to illustrate each page.

Ready for writing

Like reading, writing is a skill that develops gradually over several years. Just as children learn about reading from the time they're born, they also learn about writing from an early age by watching and imitating the people around them. When children see that writing is a way of telling people something – just like talking – they usually want to try it for themselves. It's important to encourage all their efforts, so ask them to tell you what their 'writing' says and never give them the idea that it's not real writing.

Whenever you can, let children see you writing and talk to them about what you're doing when you write a shopping list, jot down a memo or make a note on a calendar. Encourage them to include writing in their pretend play, for example by giving them a pad to use when they're playing shops, and make sure they have easy access to lots of scrap paper and a variety of pencils, pens and crayons.

You could help children to 'write' emails, letters and postcards to family members. Ask your child to tell you what to write and let them 'sign' their name.

At around the age of three, children may make their first attempts at 'writing'. This usually looks like lines of scribbles, shapes and strokes.

If children have a calendar of their own, they can cross off or colour in the days leading up to special occasions, such as birthdays, family visits or holidays.

Fingers and thumbs

To write with a pen or pencil, a child needs to be able to control very precisely the tiniest movements of their hand and fingers. These kinds of skills are known as fine motor skills. There are lots of things you can do together to help young children strengthen the muscles in their hands and fingers, and develop the fine motor skills and hand-eye co-ordination they will need for writing.

- Modelling clay or play dough is great for strengthening hand muscles. Encourage children to roll, squeeze and pinch it into different shapes.
- Lacing and stringing activities are helpful. You can buy lacing cards from good toy shops or try threading macaroni onto shoelaces.
- Look out for toys with parts that children can manipulate, such as farms, doll's houses, pegboard games, dress-up dolls and small building bricks.

Fiddly tasks, such as doing up buttons, buckles and zips, are useful for practising fine motor skills.

Art activities, such as cutting, tearing, sticking and colouring, help children to develop good hand-eye co-ordination.

To find out if a child is right- or left-handed, watch to see if they consistently use one hand rather than the other for drawing, cutting or eating.

Left or right?

Children are born either right-handed or left-handed and this normally shows at around three to five years. About ten per cent of children are left-handed, though this is much more likely if there are a lot of left-handers in your family. It's important to let children use whichever hand comes naturally to them, so always let them pick up a pencil or crayon themselves, rather than putting it into their hand. Left-handers do sometimes find writing more difficult than right-handers, but there are practical things you can do to support them (see pages 42 and 64).

Useful tip

Triangular pencils are useful for helping children, especially left-handers, to develop a good grip. You can buy these from good toy shops or art shops.

Get a grip

It's worth showing children how to hold a pen or pencil from the start, but try not to correct them constantly or you could put them off writing altogether. Their grip will usually improve naturally as they gain more control of their hand muscles. It's helpful if children are using the 'tripod' grip by the time they're five or six, as this is usually the most comfortable way to hold a pencil and it makes handwriting easier.

It's best if children write sitting in a straight-backed chair at a table, with their feet resting on the floor.

The tripod grip for right-handers

The tripod grip for left-handers

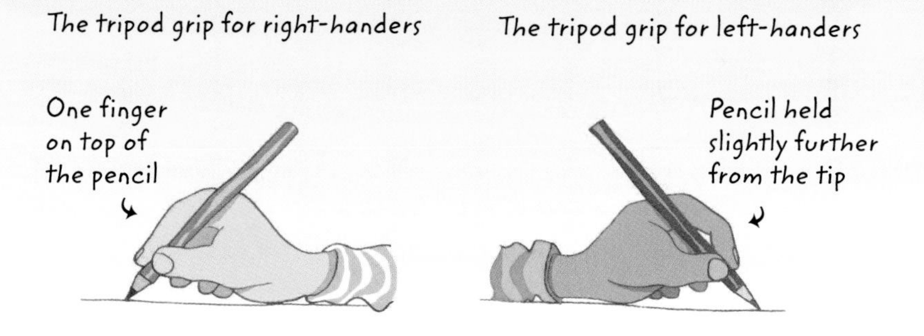

Pencil control

Children need lots of practice before they can control a pencil well enough to write legible letters. Activities such as drawing and colouring help children to improve their pencil control, as well as encouraging them to see using a pencil and paper as something fun and creative. Here are a few more ideas you can try:

Draw patterns using dotted lines or a highlighter pen and get children to trace over them in different colours.

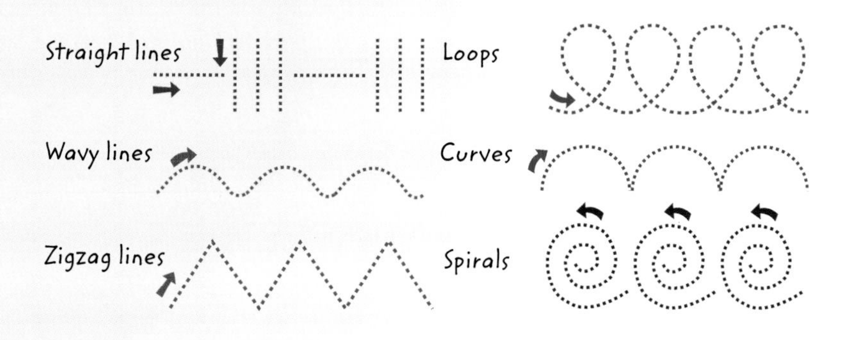

- Simple dot-to-dot books and maze activity books are a fun way to practise pencil control.
- Look out for stencils of things your child likes, such as animals or diggers, and show them how to use them.
- Try playing Noughts and Crosses together. You can get children to draw the grid for each game, as well as playing.

Forming letters

As well as being important in itself, learning how to write the letters of the alphabet is known to help children with their reading. Making the hand movements to form the letters helps them to remember what the letter shapes look like. Children learn best when they use as many different senses as possible, so encourage them to say the letter sounds out loud as they make each letter shape.

Children need to learn how to form each letter correctly right from the start. If they're left to work this out for themselves, they'll often begin the letter in the wrong place or move their hand in the wrong direction. This can cause real problems later on when children start doing joined-up writing. On page 92, you'll find a guide to show you how to form the letters correctly.

Don't expect children to learn how to write letters until they've developed reasonably good pencil control. In the meantime, there are lots of fun ways they can practise forming letters without using a pen or pencil.

1. Write some large letters on pieces of coloured card with a thick marker pen.

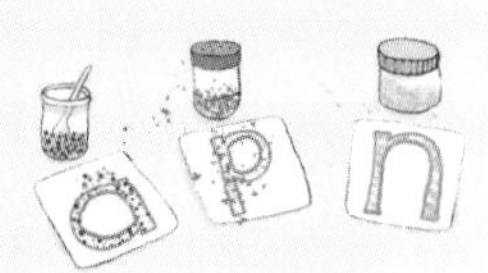

2. Squeeze glue over the letters and shake on salt, sand, glitter or sequins.

3. Once the letters are dry, ask children to trace over them with their finger.

Put some flour or rice in a baking tray and show children how to form letters with their index finger. It's best to begin with just one letter at a time.

Letter-forming activities

- Draw letters in damp sand in a sand box or on the beach.
- Tie a ribbon to a stick and write huge letters in the air.
- Make letters in finger paint spread on a washable surface.
- Breathe on a window or mirror and draw letters there.
- Trace letters on each other's back or hands.
- Use thick chalks to draw big letters on pavements or patios.

Writing letters

Once children can copy patterns and shapes using a pencil, they may be ready to start writing letters. It's easiest if they begin by tracing over letters you've drawn for them.

Useful tip

When you're writing letters for children to trace over, draw a dot to show them where each letter starts (see page 92).

Try drawing letters using faint dots for children to join up.

Let children trace over letters drawn with a highlighter pen.

Write a letter on some paper and encourage your child to copy it underneath, but keep watching to make sure they go the right way.

The next stage is to give children lots of practice in copying letters, but be careful not to turn this into a chore. It's very important that children enjoy writing, so don't push them if they're not interested. You can make letters fun by providing lots of different writing materials, such as coloured pens and pencils, crayons, chalks, glitter pens and marker pens. Remember to praise all your child's efforts – however shaky – and try not to criticize or correct them.

Writing words

A child's name is usually the first word they learn to write and it's helpful if they can do this before they start school. Once children can write all the letters in their name, you can show them their name and encourage them to copy it. When they can manage this, see if they can write it from memory. Don't worry if some of the letters are out of order or backwards, or aren't written in a straight line.

Some children may want to know how to write other favourite words, such as 'mum', 'dad' or 'cat'. Be ready to show them if they ask you, but otherwise it's fine to stick to letters and the child's own name. There'll be plenty of time for them to write words once they start school.

For children, writing their name is a huge breakthrough. Suddenly, they can sign their drawings and add their name to the bottom of cards.

Beginner readers

Once children start school, they begin the formal process of learning to read and write. This is an exciting time for your child, but learning to read is hard work, so they need lots of help and encouragement. This section explains how reading and writing are taught in schools and gives advice on how best to support children as they learn.

Key skills at a glance

Sounding out and naming the letters of the alphabet

Reading words by sounding them out and breaking words down into their separate sounds to spell them

Recognizing a growing number of words automatically on sight

Reading reasonably fluently with an adult, understanding what they read, and starting to read on their own

Developing legible handwriting, with increasing accuracy in spelling

Writing down their ideas in a way that makes sense

Enjoying books and poems, and responding to them through talking, writing and imaginative play

4 – 7 years

Learning to read

For decades, debate has raged about the best way to teach children to read. Many different methods have been devised to try to make learning easier, with supporters of one method often fiercely opposed to the others.

For many years, experts argued that children should be taught to recognize whole words, or even sentences, rather than individual letters. However, recent research shows it's crucial for children to learn the letters and the sounds they represent, so schools are now using phonics as the first step in teaching children to read words. Because English spelling is tricky, children are also taught to recognize some words on sight by seeing them over and over again. At the same time, they're introduced to a rich variety of language through books, stories, rhymes and poems.

Did you know?

Research shows that even skilled readers process all the letters and sounds in the words they read – they just do it so fast that they recognize words instantly.

What is phonics?

- Children are first taught the letters of the alphabet and the sounds they represent.
- They learn to read by 'sounding out' words letter by letter, then 'blending' the sounds together to make words.
- They learn to spell by breaking words down into their separate sounds, then writing the letters that make those sounds.

Critics claim that phonics is difficult and dull, but teachers can use lots of fun ways to help children learn letters and sounds.

What is reading?

In order to read something, you have to translate the written symbols on the page into the language that the symbols represent, and you also have to understand what the language says. For example, you may be able to 'read' the word 'limnivore', but you might not know what it means*. Your brain uses exactly the same processes to understand written language as it does to understand spoken language – the only difference is that you have to 'decode' print first to turn it into words. For this reason, a child's spoken language skills are crucial to learning to read.

- Children will understand printed words that they can decode as long as those words are already in their spoken vocabulary.

- No matter how many spoken words children know, they won't understand printed words unless they can decode them first.

Talking and reading together are great ways to boost children's vocabulary and improve their language comprehension.

Phonics first

When children begin learning to read, they first need to learn how to decode printed words. The key to decoding is being able to match the letters of the alphabet with the sounds they represent, and research shows that the best way to do this is by teaching children phonics in a systematic way from the start. Phonics teaching involves lots of talking about language and words, and this helps to enrich a child's vocabulary too. As children become better at decoding, they gradually spend less time on phonics and more time on developing their language comprehension.

Did you know?

Phonics allows children to tackle words they've never seen before and helps them to remember them, so they soon build up a store of words they recognize automatically.

* The word 'limnivore' means 'mud-eater'.

Focus on phonics

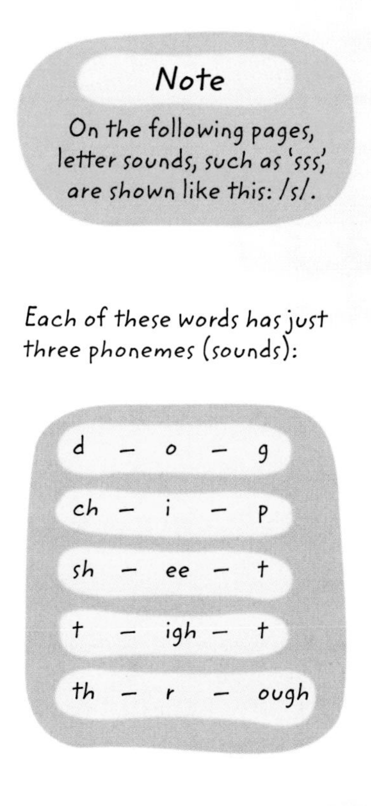

Written language is really just a complicated code that represents the words we speak. Phonics is now thought to be the best way of teaching children how to crack the code because it teaches them the connection between written letters and the sounds they stand for.

All spoken words are made up of separate sounds, called phonemes. There are about 44 different phonemes in English (you'll find a chart listing all of them on pages 90 and 91). The English alphabet only has 26 letters, so we have to use various combinations of letters to represent all 44 phonemes. Some phonemes are represented by just one letter, so the sound /s/ is represented by the letter 's'. Other sounds are represented by two, three or even four letters (you can see some examples in the panel on the left). The letters used to represent a single phoneme are called a grapheme, so 'd', 'sh', 'ee', 'igh' and 'ough' are all examples of graphemes.

Some phonics programmes use actions to help children remember the sounds made by the different graphemes.

Children begin with the sounds made by one-letter graphemes, learning up to five new letters and sounds each week. These aren't usually taught in alphabetical order, but in a way that allows children to start reading words very quickly. Different phonics programmes follow a slightly different order, but most start with 's', 'a', 't', 'p', 'i' and 'n' because you can make so many simple words with these letters. Eventually, children move on to two-letter graphemes, such as 'sh', 'ch', 'ee' and 'oa'.

You could ask your child to teach you any actions they've learned, and have fun practising them together as you say the phonemes aloud.

Fun with phonemes

Becoming familiar with all the phonemes takes more practice than children have time for in school, so your support is vital. Many schools hold a parents' evening or send out an information sheet explaining how they teach phonics and what you can do to help. For example, you might be asked to listen to a child saying sounds out loud. It's a good idea to make a note of which sounds your child is working on, so you can keep practising them at home. Young children learn best when they're having fun, so keep things playful and don't worry if some days they're too tired – just leave it for another time.

It helps if you point out words in books, food labels and road signs that include phonemes your child is learning.

Keep track of your child's progress by writing down each new phoneme they learn on a clean page of a notebook.

Try flipping regularly through the book together, getting children to say the sounds as fast as they can.

Phoneme games

- Make matching pairs of cards, with a phoneme written on one side of each card. Lay all the cards face down, then turn over two at a time to find the matching pairs.
- Put some phoneme cards into an empty tissue box, then get children to pull them out one at a time and say the sounds. Time them and see if they can beat their own time.
- Write out a bingo card showing some phonemes a child knows. Call out sounds as you pull them out of the tissue box and let the child cross them off their card.

Saying sounds

When you're practising phonemes, it's important to pronounce them as clearly and accurately as possible. Remember to say the sound that each letter makes and not its name, so say 'sss' and not 'ess'. Try to avoid saying 'uh' at the end of each consonant sound (say 'mmm' not 'muh' and 'rrr' not 'ruh') and keep sounds like /t/ and /k/ as short as possible. There's a pronunciation guide you can listen to on the Usborne Quicklinks Website (see page 84).

Useful tip

The names of the letters are often not used at all to begin with, so check the school's position on this and stick to what they advise.

Forming letters

Making the shapes of the different letters – whether on paper or in the air – helps a child to remember what they look like, so children are usually shown how to form the letters from the beginning (see page 92 for a guide to correct letter formation). Children who have just started school may find using a pencil hard work, so make things fun by getting them to practise the letter shapes in other ways (the activities on page 43 are still suitable at this stage).

Ask children to trace over letters in an ABC book with their finger, while saying the phonemes out loud.

Reading words

Once children have learned five or six letters, they're shown how to read words made up of those letters, beginning with two- and three-letter words, such as 'at', 'in', 'pat' and 'pin'. They're taught to 'sound out' each grapheme, saying the sound made by each one ('pat' is sounded out as /p/ /a/ /t/). Then they run the sounds together to make the word. This is called blending, and this way of teaching phonics is sometimes called 'synthetic' phonics, because children are taught to blend, or 'synthesize', separate sounds to read words.

At this stage, children may bring home words or short captions to sound out and blend. Make sure you give them time to work words out for themselves, encouraging them to blend the sounds all the way through the word, and let them know you're proud of their achievements.

You can practise blending by breaking words into separate sounds as you talk. Try asking children to touch their /kn/ /ee/ /s/ or /t/ /oe/ /s/.

- When you're reading aloud, stop occasionally and see if children can sound out and blend words made up of letters they know.

- Spread out some letters and point to three of them, one after the other, to make a word. See if your child can put the sounds together in their head and say the word.

Plastic magnetic letters are a great way to practise sounding out and blending.

You can start with a word such as 'sat' then swap one letter at a time to make lots of new words.

Practice makes perfect

On this page, you'll find some ways to practise the words children are working on or to revise words they've worked on before. You can add in any words you like, as long as they're made up of letters and sounds children already know. At first, they'll probably have to sound out every word, but don't make them sound out words if they don't need to. If they can blend silently or recognize a word as soon as they see it, that's great!

You could use magnetic letters to leave words on the refrigerator door for children to find when they come home from school.

Try stringing up a 'washing line' in a child's room and pegging out words made up of letters written on pieces of card. You could put up different words each day.

Word games

- Write some words on pieces of card. Put the objects that match the words (e.g. cup, tin, peg, bag) at the other side of the room. Your child has to read the word, run across the room and place the label by the right object.
- Use plastic letters to play 'Sense or nonsense'. Start with a word like 'pin' or 'rug', then ask children to change the first or last letter and decide if it makes a real word.

Some children find sounding out and blending very difficult. This isn't because they're unintelligent – they may just find it hard to remember letter shapes or have difficulty hearing the sounds in words. You can help by revising the phonemes regularly and by giving children plenty of practice at sounding out and blending. If you're at all worried, talk to their teacher.

It's important to give children lots of praise for every success, however small.

Starting to spell

Children are usually taught how to spell from the start, alongside learning to read. To spell a word, they need to hear it, break it up into individual sounds (this is called segmenting), and then remember which letters are used to represent those sounds. For example, they hear the word 'tap', break it up into the sounds /t/ /a/ /p/, and then write down the letters 't', 'a' and 'p' (you can find out more about writing on pages 64 and 65).

Plastic magnetic letters or letters written on pieces of card are ideal for practising spelling, as they're fun to play with and they allow children to spell lots of words without having to struggle with a pencil. When you're doing spelling activities, remember to stick to words made up of the letters and sounds your child knows. While children are learning individual letters, they should only be expected to read and spell two- and three-letter words. Here are a few ideas to try:

You can help children learn to segment words by playing sound games together. For example, you could say:
'Cat' is /c/ /a/ /t/
'Dog' is /d/ /o/ /?/
'Cup' is /c/ /u/ /?/

Using the 'washing line' on page 51, try getting children to peg up letters to spell words.

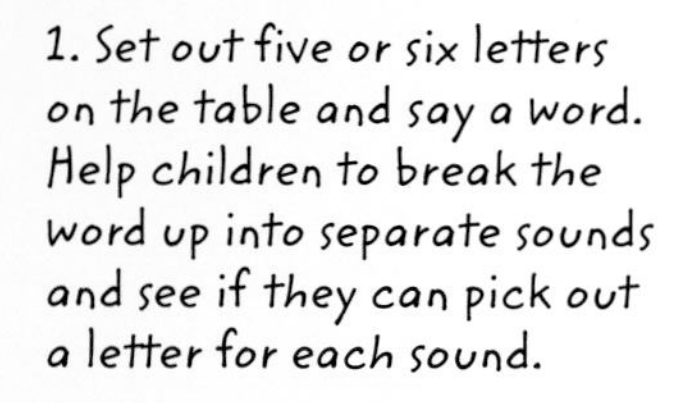

1. Set out five or six letters on the table and say a word. Help children to break the word up into separate sounds and see if they can pick out a letter for each sound.

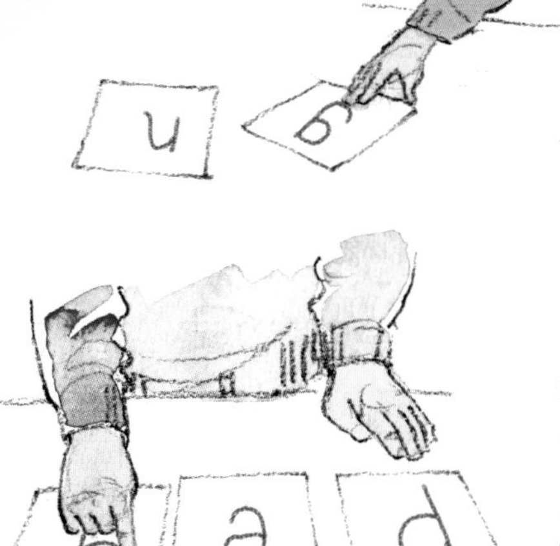

2. Once children have set out the letters to spell the word, ask them to sound it out and read it. This helps them to see how reading and spelling are linked.

Simple spelling activities

- Use letter cards or plastic letters to make a word such as 'hen', then see if a child can change it to 'pen'. Try other words, such as 'ten' or 'men'.
- Make a word such as 'sit', then ask your child to change it to 'sat', then 'rat', 'rap', 'rip', 'sip', and back to 'sit', changing one letter at a time.
- Make a word, then mix the letters up. Try saying the original word again and see if children can put the letters back in the right order.

Tricky words

Unfortunately, English has a very complicated spelling system and not all words are spelled exactly as they sound. Words like these are called irregular words or 'tricky' words and they include some of the commonest words in English. Children start learning common tricky words, such as 'to', 'the' and 'of', at an early stage. No words are completely irregular, so encourage children to sound out the regular parts of the word and help them identify the tricky part.

You can help children to remember tricky words by including them in word games.

Step by step

Phonics is usually taught in very gradual steps. It's useful if you can keep track of what stage children are at, so you don't expect them to read words that are beyond them.

At some point, children start learning sounds represented by two-letter graphemes, such as 'sh' and 'oo' (a two-letter grapheme is called a digraph). When you're practising words with digraphs, remember to sound out each grapheme, and not each letter. For example, 'thin' is sounded out as /th/ /i/ /n/ and 'rain' as /r/ /ai/ /n/.

Useful tip

If you're using plastic letters to practise digraphs, it's a good idea to tape the two letters together to make a single grapheme.

The next stage introduces combinations of consonants, such as 'sp' and 'st'. These are called consonant blends and they're different from digraphs because you can still hear the separate sounds of the individual letters. (In a digraph, such as 'sh', there is just one sound.) At this stage, children learn to tackle words such as 'spot', 'lost' and 'creeps'.

Practising consonant blends

- Try using plastic letters to make a word such as 'hum', then add a 'p' at the end and ask children what the word is now. Or add a 't' to the beginning of 'wig'.
- Playing sound games can help too. Say a word, then ask children to add a sound and identify the new word, e.g. 'The word is "lock", add /b/ and what word do you get?'

Children may enjoy string-joining puzzles, where they have to link a word with a matching picture. There are some to print out on the Usborne Quicklinks Website (see page 84).

Different spellings

1. You can help children to remember alternative spellings by making a sound book together.

2. Write one phoneme at the top of each page of a notebook, then divide the rest of the page into columns.

oo oo
moon grew clue soup
soon flew blue group
boot blew true

3. As children learn different spellings for the phonemes, they can write in examples of words with each spelling.

To begin with, children learn one grapheme for each of the 44 phonemes (for example, they learn that the sound /oo/ is spelt 'oo'). If English were like many other languages, that's all you would need. Unfortunately, things aren't quite that simple.

Most vowel sounds in English can be spelled in several different ways. The words 'moon', 'blue', 'grew' and 'soup' all include the phoneme /oo/, but it's spelled either 'oo', 'ue', 'ew' or 'ou'. Not only that, but most graphemes can be pronounced in more than one way. The words 'though', 'bough', 'rough' and 'cough' all contain the grapheme 'ough', but it's pronounced differently in each word.

As children progress, they're gradually introduced to many of these alternative spellings and pronunciations. When they're reading, they're taught to try out one pronunciation of a word, then try another if the first sounds wrong or doesn't make sense. Once children understand the basic rules of phonics, they're often able to go beyond what they've been taught and work out some of these alternatives for themselves.

Practising pronunciation

1. Make some cards showing words that have the same grapheme, but are pronounced differently, e.g. 'how' 'now' 'brown' 'cow' and 'mow' 'blow' 'grow' 'show'.

2. Shuffle the cards and ask children to sort them into two piles according to how they're pronounced (see the Usborne Quicklinks Website for more examples of suitable words).

Children's ability to read usually outstrips their ability to spell, so even if they can read words with alternative spellings, they may not be able to write them accurately.

Faster word reading

Phonics is just the first step in learning to read fluently. Once children have sounded out and blended a word several times, they'll start to recognize the word automatically as soon as they see it, without having to sound it out. This is what you want, so don't make children sound out words unless they get stuck or get a word wrong.

With practice, the number of words a child can read on sight gradually increases. This is a process that continues throughout a person's life – even well-read adults occasionally come across words they've never seen before! On this page, you'll find some ideas to give children extra practice in word reading. The activities can easily be adapted to make them easier or harder – just remember to choose words your child can manage.

1. To play 'Stepping stones', write words on big circles of paper, then lay them on the floor and call out instructions, such as 'Jump on "boat"!'

2. You can extend this by including verbs and other parts of speech. See if your child can jump from word to word to make a sentence.

You could make up a treasure hunt, with a list of things to find around the house, and see how quickly children can collect all the items.

1. Turn speedy reading into a game by writing some words on cards and putting them in an empty tissue box.

2. Then set a kitchen timer and see how many words children can pull out and read in a minute.

Word-reading activities

- Picture word lotto is a fun way to practise reading words.
- Play 'Snap' using word cards instead of picture cards.
- Use pairs of word cards to play the pairs game on page 49.
- Point out regular words on signs, posters and labels.

Becoming fluent

Did you know?

• Reading out loud helps beginner readers to connect letters and sounds, and to blend the sounds into words they can recognize.

• The more children read, the more words they come across. The more often they see these words, the faster they're able to read them.

To become fluent readers, children need to be able to recognize words quickly, effortlessly and accurately. It takes years to become a really fluent reader and needs lots of practice – the more children read, the better they become. Beginner readers learn best if they read with an adult, so the most important thing you can do is to spend time listening to children as they read. They need to read books that are reasonably easy for them, and teachers have lots of experience in providing children with reading material at the right level for their age and abilities. Ideally, a child should be getting no more than one word in 20 wrong.

Beginner readers need lots of reassurance. Reading simple books gives them the confidence to tackle harder ones later on.

To help your child feel relaxed about reading, find a quiet place, without any distractions, and let them snuggle up close to you.

Useful tip

Remember to keep reading aloud to your child. It shows them what fluent reading sounds like and reminds them how much fun reading can be.

To begin with, your child may bring home words, captions or sentences to read, before moving on to simple books. Most schools use a graded reading scheme, with children choosing their own books from a selection that's right for them and moving through different levels as they progress. Increasingly, schools are using schemes that tie in with the phonics skills children have been learning. These kinds of books are called 'decodable' books, because in the early stages they're mostly made up of phonically regular words that children can decode by sounding them out.

Reading together

If possible, try to set aside about 10 minutes each day to listen to your child read. Reading is hard work for young children and they won't be able to concentrate for much longer than this, so little and often is best. Choose a time when your child isn't too tired and when you can give them your full attention.

Starting to read is very exciting for children, so be enthusiastic about their reading, no matter how simple the books they bring home. Beginner readers usually read very slowly, one word at a time, so try to be patient and remember to give them lots of praise and encouragement, even if they don't get everything right first time (you can find out more about correcting mistakes on page 58).

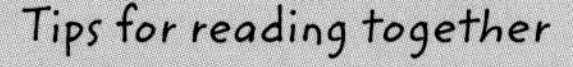

Tips for reading together

- Encourage children to run their finger under the words as they read.
- Make it fun by looking at the pictures and talking about the book together as you go along (see page 63 for more on this).
- If children are reluctant to read, try taking it in turns to read a sentence, a paragraph or a page at a time.
- If your child is getting tired, bored or frustrated, then it's time to stop.
- Re-reading books helps children to read more fluently, so let them read their favourites again and again.

It's vital that dads or other male relatives listen to children read, otherwise boys especially can get the idea that reading is just for girls.

- Once children have read a book a few times with you, they might be ready to have a go at reading it on their own.
- Try encouraging beginner readers to read to younger children – it will make them feel very grown up!

Correcting mistakes

If children make a mistake when they're reading aloud, try not to jump in too quickly – they may spot the mistake themselves if you give them time. If the mistake makes sense, let your child read to the end of the page, then ask them to go back and try the word again, looking at all the letters, and sounding it out if they need to. If the mistake doesn't make sense – and your child hasn't noticed – it's best to stop straight away. You can help children learn to correct their own mistakes by asking questions, such as 'Does that sound right?' or 'Did that make sense?'

Dealing with mistakes

- Correct children gently and with lots of encouragement, for example, 'You're doing really well, but have another look at that word.'

- Do all you can to build your child's confidence – don't dwell on their mistakes and never tell them they're stupid or not trying hard enough.

- If your child is getting more than one word in 20 wrong, gently steer them to an easier book or read it to them all the way through first.

Children need to feel they're succeeding, even if they're making lots of mistakes, so make sure you always find something to praise.

Getting stuck

Sometimes, children may just get stuck on an unfamiliar word. When this happens, encourage them to sound the word out. If it's an irregular word, help them to identify the tricky part and talk about how it sounds. Remember to give them lots of praise if they get the word right – or even try to. If you have to stop to focus on a word, it's a good idea for the child to go back and re-read the whole sentence, so they don't lose the meaning of what they've read.

As children become more fluent, they gradually learn faster ways of working out unfamiliar words. The panel on the left gives some examples of techniques you could try.

Tackling longer words

- To help children work out longer words, try clapping out the number of syllables, for example 'an-i-mal.'

- Encourage children to look for smaller words they know inside longer words, for example, spotting 'eat' in 'eaten' or 'help' in 'helpful.'

- Help children to see how words are built up using different endings and beginnings, for example, 'play,' 'playing,' 'played' and 'replay.'

Spotting problems

Do try not to worry if your child's progress seems slow. Reading is hard and children may improve only in fits and starts. However, if your child is really struggling to read the books they bring home from school, it's a good idea to let their teacher know. The teacher will be able to reassure you, suggest ways you can help or, if necessary, get your child any extra support they need. There's more advice about reading difficulties on pages 81 to 83.

Useful tip

If children are finding reading hard, try to build their confidence by reminding them of other things they're good at.

Books for beginners

You can inspire beginner readers to practise by letting them see you reading for pleasure too – and by giving them lots of easy, enjoyable books to read. To begin with, go for books with clear type, just one or two lines of text per page, and lots of colourful illustrations that bring the text to life. It's best if children choose their own books, but you may need to help them pick books that aren't too hard for them – they should be able to read a book with just a little help from you. Below are a few ideas that might appeal.

If you can, take children to the library regularly – it's a great way for them to sample a wide variety of books.

Books with rhyming text made up of familiar letters and sounds

Simple non-fiction books on topics your child is interested in

Activity books with step-by-step instructions and helpful pictures

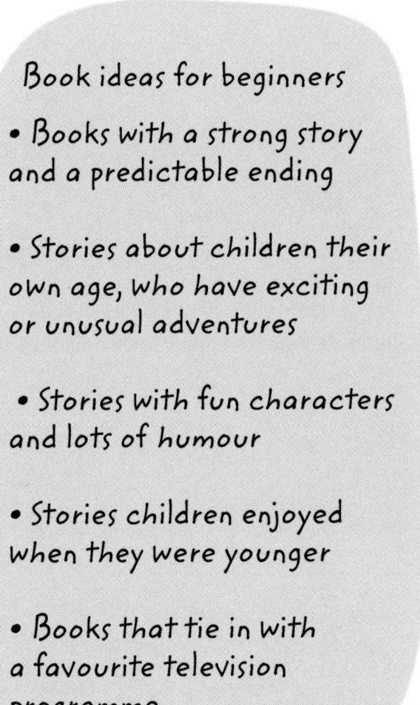

Book ideas for beginners

- Books with a strong story and a predictable ending
- Stories about children their own age, who have exciting or unusual adventures
- Stories with fun characters and lots of humour
- Stories children enjoyed when they were younger
- Books that tie in with a favourite television programme

Key factors in good reading comprehension

- Good word-reading skills
- Good spoken language skills
- Wide general knowledge
- Familiarity with books, print and story structure

Getting the message

Reading involves much more than just being able to recognize words – children also need to understand what they read. If they're reading the words without getting the meaning, then they're not really reading at all. On the other hand, once children can decode words quickly and accurately, they can focus all their attention on understanding what they're reading.

Reading comprehension depends on a whole range of different skills, knowledge and experiences (see the panel above left) and it develops alongside the ability to read words. On the next few pages, you'll find lots of ways to help your child improve their comprehension skills while they're learning to read.

Tips for talking

- As you chat, introduce new and interesting words whenever you can.
- Tell children what new words mean and repeat them often in conversations.
- Don't simplify your language too much – children need to hear complex sentences.

Keep talking

Spoken language is the basis for reading comprehension – if children don't understand language that they hear, they won't understand it when they read it. Good readers need to have a wide spoken vocabulary and know how words fit together to make sentences that mean something. Until children can read for themselves, they mostly learn new words through conversations, especially with adults, and by listening to adults read to them.

It's important to talk to your child as much as you can. Mealtimes are an opportunity to share conversations about the day that's past.

Words, words, words

Talking to children about words as they crop up in conversation is a natural way to build their vocabulary and make them more aware of language. You can explain how related words have similar meanings, for example 'science' and 'scientist', and how parts of words can change a word's meaning, as in 'helpful' and 'helpless' or 'undo' and 'redo'. Point out words, such as 'mind' and 'light', that have more than one meaning. Encourage children to ask about words they don't understand, then look them up in a dictionary together and read out the definition.

Fun with words

- Together, see how many words you can think of with the same meaning, e.g. 'yummy', 'tasty', 'delicious', 'mouthwatering'.

- Choose a category, such as fruits, vehicles or kinds of buildings, and see how many words you can think of in that category.

- Encourage children to play with words by telling them jokes with puns and making up silly rhymes and tongue twisters.

Cooking, baking and craft activities are great ways to introduce new words for tools, ingredients and making things.

Invest in a very simple first dictionary and show your child how to look up words.

The wider world

Good readers draw on their own experiences and their knowledge of the world around them to make sense of what they're reading, so expanding your child's general knowledge will really help their reading comprehension. Outings to museums, castles, wildlife parks, or even the local park, provide ideal opportunities for children to learn new things. Non-fiction books, educational television programmes, websites and DVD-ROMs are also great sources of information, but bear in mind that children who can't yet read on their own will need a lot of support.

When you take children out, talk to them about everything you see and do.

Reading to children

Reading should be fun, so let children choose what to read and don't insist on finishing a book they're not enjoying.

It's vital to keep reading aloud to your child while they're learning to read. By listening to you read, they'll hear more complex language than they do in everyday conversations, they'll become familiar with a wider range of writing styles and story patterns, and they'll broaden their knowledge of the world around them. All of this will help them to make sense of books that they eventually read on their own.

Ideally, you should read as many different kinds of books as you can, from factual books and realistic fiction to adventure stories, fantasy and poetry. Don't worry, though, if your child prefers one type of book and dislikes another – the main thing is to read books children enjoy. Try stories about characters they can identify with and point them towards non-fiction books that match their interests. Magazines about sports or hobbies may go down well too.

School-age children can concentrate for longer periods, so you should be able to read for 15 or 20 minutes at a time. Rather than reading two short books, go for longer, more complex picture books and books with chapters that can be read over several days or weeks. The idea is to read books that are more advanced than children can read themselves.

Series of books that feature the same character involved in different adventures are very popular at this age.

As your child's reading develops, you could take turns reading a paragraph at a time.

It might be fun for your child to take the part of one of the characters.

Useful tip

There are links to lists of recommended books on the Usborne Quicklinks Website (see page 84).

Talking about books

To make sense of a book, good readers think constantly about what they're reading. They notice when something doesn't make sense and know to go back and look at that part again. They make links between their own experiences and what they read in books and can 'read between the lines' to work out what's really going on. They think about what might happen next or how a story might end. You can help children to develop these skills by encouraging them to talk about books you read together (see the panel on the right for a few ideas on what to talk about).

Before you begin reading, see if children can remember what happened in the previous chapter. It's best if you then allow them to get immersed in the story and leave talking about it until afterwards, but do respond if they make a comment, and encourage them to ask about anything they don't understand.

Talking about books

- Ask about the characters – why they act as they do, how they're feeling and what you would do in their place.
- Stop at a suspenseful point and ask what might happen next. Imagine what might happen after the book ends.
- Link events and characters in books to your child's experiences and to books you've read in the past.
- Talk about which bits of a book you both liked best, or which bits were funniest, scariest or most exciting.

Dressing up and acting out stories they've read is great fun and helps children to learn about how a story is put together.

- Do a quiz by taking turns to ask each other questions about a book. The first to get five right answers is the winner.
- Read a story, then watch a DVD of the book (or the other way around) and talk about the similarities and differences.
- Encourage children to re-tell stories they've had read to them in school or ones they've watched on television.

Learning to write

It's common for children to write some letters back to front. This usually sorts itself out by the age of six or seven.

There is a close link between learning to read and learning to write. The two skills develop together and build on one another, so helping children with their writing also helps their reading – and vice versa. Writing is the most difficult language skill children have to master, involving a whole range of separate skills, such as handwriting, spelling and use of language, as well as planning what to say. It takes several years to learn to write accurately, so give your child lots of encouragement and don't expect too much too soon.

Handwriting hints

Left-handed children may find it easier to write on a slope, with the paper at a 45 degree angle to their body.

By the time they're five, most children will have settled on which hand to use for writing. Whether they're left- or right-handed, they'll find writing easier if they hold their pencil comfortably (see page 42). Learning to control a pencil is hard for young children, so don't worry if their writing is messy at first – it will get neater as their fine motor skills develop. For now, it's more important that they're forming the letters correctly (see page 92). It's a good idea to talk to your child's teacher about this, as some schools teach a version of joined-up writing from the start.

Make writing fun by providing different writing materials, such as coloured pens and pencils, glitter pens, crayons and chalks.

Practising handwriting

- Let children trace over letters you've drawn in dotted lines or with a highlighter pen.
- Call out letter sounds and ask your child to write down each letter as they hear it.
- Play games, such as seeing how many letter 'd's your child can write in a minute.

Learning to spell

When children first start to write, they spell words the way they hear them, often without any vowels, for example 'dk' instead of 'duck'. As they learn more about letters and sounds, they're gradually able to write down all the sounds in a word, so 'dk' becomes 'duk'.

At this stage, it's helpful to play lots of simple spelling games, but don't push young children into doing these activities if they're not interested. A wipe-clean board, such as a kitchen memo board, is ideal for practising spelling. Ask your child to write a word, such as 'bug', then get them to change it to 'rug', 'rag', 'bag', and so on, by changing just one letter at a time.

Useful tip

To spell a word, encourage your child to say the word, listen to all the sounds in it and write down a letter, or group of letters, for each sound.

Spelling games

- Play 'Hangman' with simple three-letter words. You can find out how to play on the Usborne Quicklinks Website (see page 84).
- Write a few words on pieces of paper. Let children look, then turn them over and see if they can write the words down from memory.
- See if your child can put words in alphabetical order based on their first letter, e.g. 'cat', 'fat', 'hat', 'mat'.

When you start doing spelling activities, make sure you choose words that are spelled exactly as they sound.

Write down a word, then cut the letters apart and see if your child can put them back in the right order.

During their first year at school, children also begin learning how to spell common 'tricky' words, such as 'the', 'are' and 'was'. Gradually, they develop a bank of words they write often and can spell the right way. To help children remember tricky words, point them out whenever you come across them and include them in spelling games.

Better spelling

Once children start learning that sounds can be spelled in more than one way, as in 'too', 'blue' and 'flew', their spelling gradually becomes more accurate, but it's a slow process. You can help by pointing out words with similar spellings, for example by making lists of words with the same letter pattern, such as 'pail', 'mail', 'tail' or 'fetch', 'ditch', 'hatch', and so on. See how many words the two of you can write down in a minute and let children highlight the letter pattern in a different colour.

When children bring home spellings to learn, it's best if they write the words down. Most schools teach children to look at the word, then cover it up, write it down from memory and check it (the 'Look, Cover, Write and Check' method). Children do need to learn how to spell correctly, but it's important not to turn writing and spelling into a chore, or you could put them off completely. If your child is tired after school, it's better to leave it than push too hard for now. Spelling games and puzzles can be a fun way to give children extra practice.

Ask children to find and circle words in magazines with a particular letter pattern.

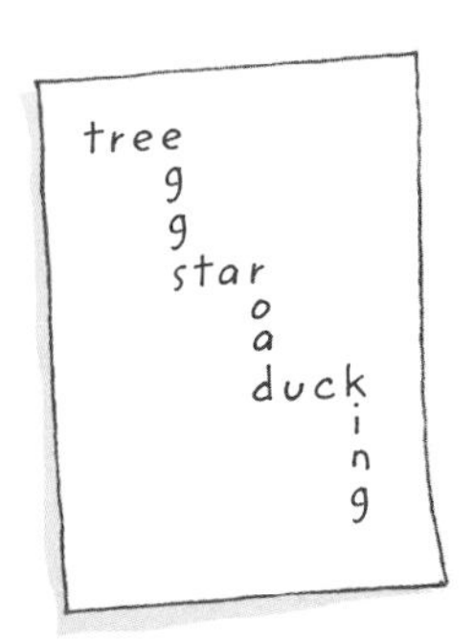

Word staircases are fun to make. Try three- or four-letter words and take turns to think of the next word.

More spelling games

- Write silly sentences together using words children need to learn.
- Write down a word, such as 'sandwich,' and see how many other words your child can make from it ('hand,' 'chin,' 'saw,' 'dish,' and so on).
- Write a word one letter at a time and see how quickly children can guess the word. Let them write down words for you to guess.

Simple crossword puzzles, word searches and anagrams can all help children to look more closely at words.

Independent writing

From the start, children are encouraged to write on their own whenever they want to. At first, they make up their own spellings based on how words sound, for example 'I luv yoo mumee'. The most helpful thing you can do at this stage is to encourage your child to experiment. Give them lots of praise and talk to them about what their writing says. Don't correct their spelling, but do suggest they put a space between each word to make it easier to read.

Useful tip

If you have difficulty deciphering what young children have written, you could ask them to read it out to you.

You can show children you value their writing by sticking their labelled pictures on the wall or collecting their stories in a scrapbook.

Helping with writing

- Say your thoughts out loud as you write things down, so children can see how you put your ideas on paper.
- Encourage children to think about what they want to say before they try to write it down.
- Suggest children re-read what they've written. Are they happy with it? Do they want to change anything?
- Help children to check words they're not sure of in a simple first dictionary.

As children's spelling improves, they'll start asking for help with words they don't know. Encourage them to have a go themselves and suggest some ways to tackle words they're not sure of (see page 75), then help them with any tricky parts. You could now start to correct your child's spelling, but be sensitive and don't discourage them by pointing out every mistake – just pick out one or two words at a time. What children write is just as important as how it's spelled, so be enthusiastic about the content and praise them for any interesting words they've used.

Reading to children is a huge help because it gives them a model for how good writing should sound.

Encouraging writing

The most important thing you can do to help children with their writing is to encourage them to write, so they really enjoy putting their ideas down on paper. When you can, include your child in everyday writing activities, such as helping with a shopping list or writing a note, and create opportunities for them to write on their own – anything from birthday cards and invitations to postcards, thank-you notes, and letters or emails to family.

Useful tip

It's helpful if your child has a special place to write, with lots of paper and pens to hand.

You could hang up a family messageboard and leave each other notes.

Give children a calendar where they can write in special events.

Encourage children to include writing in their pretend play.

You can encourage children's storytelling by making up stories together. Try inventing new adventures for a favourite character in a book and take turns adding to the story. Tell your child stories about when you were younger and ask them to describe funny or exciting things that have happened to them. Encourage them to write their stories down and illustrate them. If children are reluctant, suggest they write about something they're really interested in, such as dinosaurs, firefighters or rockets.

Writing ideas

- Help your child to start a diary. Explain what it's for and talk about the kinds of things they might write in it.
- Suggest children make a holiday scrapbook. They can stick in photos, drawings and tickets, and label them.
- Encourage your child to make a 'Book about Me' (what I look like, my pets, family, hobbies, and so on).

You could help children to make their own book by punching holes in some paper and tying the sheets together with ribbon.

Young readers

As children's reading becomes more fluent, they start to enjoy reading quietly on their own. They're still learning the skills they will need to become confident readers and writers, and this section suggests some ways you can help. Most important of all is to encourage children to read for pleasure, so they develop a love of reading that will last a lifetime.

Key skills at a glance

Recognizing most common words on sight and knowing how to tackle longer, unfamiliar words

Reading silently for pleasure and reading aloud fluently

Thinking about what they read, noticing how well they've understood something and 'reading between the lines'

Being able to find information using indexes, glossaries, dictionaries, computers and libraries

Spelling most common words accurately and being able to use basic punctuation

Knowing how to plan, revise and proofread their own writing

Developing reading skills

By around the age of seven, most children will be able to read some books on their own. Their reading will start to speed up as they recognize more words on sight, though they'll still hesitate over unfamiliar words, using their phonics skills to help them. It's still a good idea to listen to your child read each day, as this will help them to read more fluently and expressively. At this stage, it can be fun to share the reading. You could take turns to read a page each or one of you could take the part of the narrator while the other reads the dialogue. Listening to you read will help your child to learn how fluent reading should sound.

Note

Not all children will be reading on their own at seven and some may still be struggling. If your child is finding reading difficult, you'll find some advice on pages 81 to 83.

Children generally enjoy being read to long after they are able to read on their own.

Once children can read confidently, they may prefer to read on their own. Don't insist on them doing shared reading if they'd rather not.

When children are reading on their own, they'll inevitably come across words they won't recognize straight away. They may ask you for help but, rather than just telling them the word, it's best if you encourage them to have a go at working it out for themselves. By now, they may be relying less on sounding out words letter by letter and should be able to recognize sequences of letters at a time. On the left, you'll find some of the approaches they'll have been taught at school. Remember to give your child lots of praise for any attempts they make at deciphering a word.

Tackling unfamiliar words

- Break words down into smaller chunks, such as 'or-gan-ic' or 'phar-ma-cy', and sound out the chunks.
- Look for words you know inside longer words, such as 'know' inside 'knowledge'.
- Look for parts of words that you recognize, such as 're-' in 'reappear', 'un-' in 'unable' or '-less' in 'careless'.
- Read to the end of the sentence and ask 'What word would make sense?'

Reading to learn

As children's reading progresses, they gradually make the transition from learning to read to 'reading to learn'. In other words, they no longer read simply to practise reading, but to find out information – and for fun. As children read more, so their vocabulary and general knowledge expands. This in turn makes them better readers, so the more they read, the better they become.

At school and for homework, children will be expected to read more complex material and will be assessed on how much they've learned from it, rather than on how well they've read it. They need to learn to 'listen' carefully to what they're reading, so they can tell if it makes sense to them. If they don't understand something, suggest they go back and re-read it slowly. Help them to look up unfamiliar words in the book's glossary or in a dictionary.

Increasingly, children will be expected to 'read between the lines' to work out what a writer is trying to say. To help them get the most out of what they're reading, encourage them to ask themselves questions as they read (see the panel above right for some ideas).

Thinking about books

- Who is telling the story?
- Why did X do that? How does X feel?
- What does the writer think about...?
- Can I imagine what that looks like?
- How does that tie in with what I already know?
- How would I say that in my own words?
- What's the main thing I've learned about...?

The internet can be a fantastic resource for school projects, but children will need help to find websites with suitable information at the right level.

Invest in a good junior dictionary, one that includes example sentences showing how words are used.

Useful tip

Show children how to use the contents page, index and headings in books to find the information they need.

Encouraging reading

It sounds obvious, but if children are to become lifelong readers, they need to enjoy reading. Because they have to read so much at school and for homework, there's a danger they may start to see it as a chore, so you have a vital part to play in encouraging them to read for fun.

Children are much more likely to enjoy reading if they're allowed to read whatever they want; you can suggest reading material they might like, but let them choose. Show them how to decide if a particular book is right for them, for example by looking at the front cover and the blurb on the back, then reading a few pages. And remember that children don't just have to read books – it doesn't matter what they read as long as they enjoy it.

Encouraging reading

- Make sure children have time to read, for example 20 minutes before school, after dinner or at bedtime.
- Aim to set aside times when the whole family can read quietly together.
- Create a quiet, comfy place at home where your child can curl up with a book.
- Let children read their favourite books again and again if they want to.

Take your child to the library often and show them how to find books about things that interest them.

Multimedia, such as DVDs, DVD-ROMs and the internet, are great for engaging children's interest. Boys especially may prefer reading text on screen to reading a book, while watching a film on DVD can be a way in to reading the book it was based on. You can help children to find suitable websites about their hobbies and interests, or their favourite authors, and show them how to scan a page to locate the information they want.

Ideas for reading material

- Children's fiction
- Factual books
- Encyclopedias
- Joke books
- Poems
- Annuals
- Craft and activity books
- Cookbooks
- Books that tie in with films or television programmes
- Magazines (consider buying a subscription for your child)
- Comics
- Graphic novels
- Newspapers (the sports pages are often popular)
- Catalogues
- Song lyrics
- Websites
- Emails
- DVD-ROMs

Taking an interest

Children will be more motivated to read if they feel that their reading is valued, so take an interest in whatever they're reading – even if it doesn't appeal to you – and talk to them about it. You could ask them what they're reading at the moment, what it's about and if it's any good. Ask them what they like about it and encourage them to read out any bits they particularly enjoyed. Never dismiss what your child is reading as 'rubbish' or 'just a comic'.

You could ask children to tell you their top five favourite reads and why they like them.

Be a role model

Research shows that children are much more likely to read if they see the adults around them reading. This is especially true for boys, who may lose interest unless they can see that their dads, uncles or granddads value and enjoy reading. Try to find time to read for pleasure yourself and talk to your child about what you're reading. Point out interesting headlines or articles in newspapers and magazines, explain any issues they raise, and ask children what they think. It also helps if you include children in everyday activities that involve reading. You could look at a television guide together to plan what to watch or make something by following a set of instructions.

Reading activities

- Follow a recipe and cook a meal together.
- Read film reviews and decide which film to watch.
- Look at holiday brochures or websites together if you're planning a trip.
- Take a field guide when you go for a walk and see how many different wildflowers, birds or trees you can spot.

Encourage your child to pick up a book at any time during the day, but don't worry if they only read at bedtime.

Developing writing skills

Create a word pyramid by starting with a two-letter word, then taking turns to add one letter at a time.

Draw a grid of nine letters and see how many words your child can make using each letter only once in each word.

Writing is an integral part of every subject that children will learn at school, so if they're to succeed it's vital that they develop good writing skills. By the time they start secondary school, they need to be able to write and spell words almost automatically, so they can concentrate on thinking about what they want to say.

It's much harder to spell words than it is to read them. To read a word, you just need to be able to recognize it, but to spell it, you have to remember all the letters in the word without seeing it. So although your child may be reading quite fluently at seven, it will take a few more years before they'll be able to spell accurately. In the meantime, they'll still invent spellings for words they're not sure of.

English spelling is particularly difficult, so children need lots of practice – and lots of encouragement.

Children are more likely to become good spellers if they're interested in words, so have fun together with jokes, puns and tongue twisters. Word games, like the ones on this page, are great for encouraging an interest in language and are an enjoyable way for children to practise spelling (see also page 66 – the games and activities suggested there can easily be adapted for this age group).

Word games

- Create a word chain where you use the last two letters of a word to start the next (e.g. apple – lean – angel).
- On car journeys, make up words from the registration plates of cars you pass (e.g. 'SLE' makes 'slice' or 'sleep').
- Make a secret code by giving each letter of the alphabet a number. Write messages for each other to decode.
- Commercial games, such as those that use letter tiles, cards or dice, are a good investment.

Having a go

It's important that children have the confidence to tackle words they're not sure of. This won't happen if you pick them up on every mistake, so be sensitive, especially if they find spelling hard. If your child asks you how to spell a word, encourage them to have a go themselves and remind them to try the strategies they've been taught at school (see the panel below right). Remember to give them lots of praise if they make a good attempt at a word.

To help them tackle new words, children are taught how to build words by putting two words together, such as 'play' and 'ground' to make 'playground'. They learn to add prefixes (such as 'dis-', 're-' and 'un-') to the beginning of a word and suffixes (such as '-less', '-ly' and '-ful') to the end. You can practise word building by writing down a word, such as 'happy', then seeing how many words you can make together by adding prefixes and suffixes, for example 'unhappy', 'happily', 'happiness' and 'unhappiness'. Or write down a word, such as 'day', and see how many words you can make by combining it with other words ('daytime', 'daybreak', 'birthday', 'weekday', and so on).

Children need to feel safe about trying new words, otherwise they'll just get stuck when they come to a word they can't spell.

It's useful if you help children to look up words they can't spell in a junior dictionary.

Tackling spellings

- Break words down into chunks (e.g. dra-gon-fly) and listen for the sounds in each chunk.
- Does the word contain any smaller words you already know (e.g. 'care-less')?
- Think of spelling patterns in words you know (e.g. to spell 'fright,' think of 'night,' 'light' and 'tight').
- Think of words you know with a similar meaning (e.g. 'know' and 'knowledge').
- Try the word out on a scrap of paper. Does it look right? Which part looks wrong? Try a different spelling.

Learning spellings

Children do need to know how to spell accurately and will probably bring home lists of words to learn. Some schools use a spelling log to keep a record of particular words that each child needs to focus on. Encourage your child to copy out words they need to learn, as studies have shown that writing spellings down helps children to remember them. Most schools teach the 'Look, Cover, Write and Check' method (see page 66). On the left are some suggestions for how to help your child remember words they find difficult.

Remembering spellings

- Say the word as it's written (e.g. Wed-nes-day).
- Link the word with words that look similar (e.g. 'here, there and everywhere').
- Link the word with words that have a similar meaning (e.g. 'sign' and 'signal').
- Think up mnemonics for hard spellings (e.g. 'a dessert with two spoons' reminds you that 'dessert' has two 's's).

You could ask children to write a paragraph using the words they have to learn. It can be as silly as they like.

Encourage children to look at words carefully and point out words they're learning when you come across them in books you read together. Playing games with words they need to learn will also help children to remember them.

Spelling games

- Let children key their spellings into a mobile phone as a text message. (Make sure you turn off predictive text first.)
- Ask children to write their spellings on slips of paper. How fast can they put the words in alphabetical order?
- Use a finger to spell a word on your child's back and see if they can identify it. Then let them try spelling a word.
- Using a kitchen timer, time children to see how fast they can look up their spellings in a dictionary.

1. Your child could use a notebook to make their own spelling dictionary of words they find hard to remember.

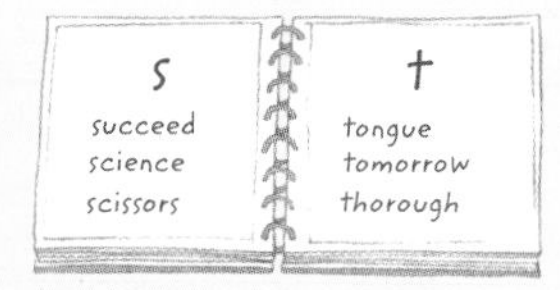

2. They could use a page for each letter of the alphabet and add in new words as they come across them.

The writing process

It's tempting just to comment on children's spelling and punctuation when they show you their work, but remember that what they write and how they go about it are just as important as the way the words are spelled.

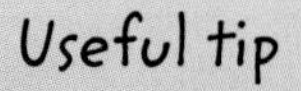

Invest in a children's thesaurus and show your child how to find interesting words to use in their writing.

Before your child starts writing, encourage them to talk about what they want to say and let them jot down some ideas first, as this will help them to organize their thoughts. It's a good idea if they then write a rough draft which they can re-read and revise. At this stage, ignore any spelling mistakes and help them to think about the content of what they've written. Is it clear? Does it make sense? How does it make you feel as a reader? Can you make any links with your child's experiences or books they've read? Try to phrase your comments as questions, rather than criticisms, and give children lots of praise for any original ideas or interesting words they've used.

Writing requires a lot of concentration. Children have to plan what they're going to say, as well as thinking about spelling and punctuation.

Once children are happy with the content of their writing, help them to proofread it, checking for spelling and punctuation mistakes. They can then produce a final, neat copy.

Using computers

- Computer software is ideal for revising content, as text can easily be changed and moved around.
- Spellcheckers can be useful, but children need to be shown how to use them properly.
- Software packages give a professional-looking finish, which can be very motivating for children.
- Encourage your child to experiment with different fonts, colours and layouts.

Encouraging writing

Children often have limited choice about the topics they write about for school, so they need to be free to write whatever they want at home. You can suggest fun projects to do, but let them choose. Be enthusiastic about their writing and show them how much you value it by finding a way to store or display pieces they're proud of.

It's helpful if you can provide a wide selection of colourful paper, notebooks and folders, as well as a variety of pens and pencils.

Collect pieces of writing in an album or scrapbook or photocopy special pieces to send to family members.

Remember to let children see you writing whenever you can and involve them in everyday writing tasks. When you're making a shopping list, you could call out the items for them to write down. They could also make lists of what to take on holiday or wish lists for birthday presents. Leave a notepad near the phone so your child can take down messages and give them a diary so they can keep a note of parties, holidays and special events. They might like to have their own address book too.

Writing ideas

- Keep a holiday journal. Describe what you do each day and stick in photos, tickets and leaflets.
- Use a computer to make a family newspaper or magazine and distribute it to friends and relatives.
- Make a time capsule. Write about the past year (best bits, worst bits, places you visited, hobbies etc.). Add photos and store in a safe place.
- Write out a play or puppet show to perform with friends. Make posters, tickets and programmes for the show.
- Write a story about what happens after the end of a book you've read.
- Design a menu for a special meal and make place cards for the guests.

Encourage children to write letters or emails to relatives or to their favourite author (you can often find the address on an author's website).

Useful information

This part of the book has more information that you might find useful as a parent or carer. There's such a vast amount of material available about all aspects of children's literacy – on the internet, in books, magazines and so on – that it can seem overwhelming. You might like to use these suggestions as a starting point.

What will I find here?

Advice on supporting bi-lingual children and children who are learning an additional language

Suggestions on how to help reluctant readers and children with literacy difficulties

Information about useful websites to visit

Literacy development charts so you can see at a glance what children might be doing at certain ages

Charts showing the phonemes (sounds) in the English language and how to form the letters of the alphabet

Other languages

Many children grow up speaking more than one language. Some learn two languages directly from their parents, while others speak one or two languages at home, then pick up a second or third language when they start school or preschool. A child may be equally fluent in two – or even three – languages or may be stronger in one than another. Each child's situation is unique.

It's important that children feel proud of the language, or languages, they speak at home.

Bi-lingual children

If you are bringing your child up to be bi-lingual, it's usually best for each parent to stick to just one language, as this helps children to keep the two languages separate. Don't worry, though, if young children sometimes use words from both languages in the same sentence. This is perfectly normal and will sort itself out.

If one of your child's languages is the one they will use at school, then they will learn to read quite normally without any extra support. Bi-lingual children are usually more aware of language than other children and there is some evidence that they actually learn to read faster, especially if their two languages share the same alphabet. The best way to support your child is to spend time talking and reading to them in all the ways suggested in this book – but do it in both their languages. Do make sure your child's school knows that you are bringing them up bi-lingually.

An additional language

If the language you speak at home is not the one your child will use at school, then they will have to learn a new language when they start school. In the case of English, this is known as learning English as an Additional Language (or EAL).

Don't worry if your child is in this situation – until around the age of seven, children learn new languages fairly easily. They'll begin to pick up the second language if they attend a toddler group, nursery or preschool, and their language skills will be assessed when they start school. At that point, they'll be entitled to extra language support if they need it. It's important that children learn to speak the second language before learning to read it.

If you don't speak the language your child uses at school, here are some ways you can support them as they learn to read and write:

- Spend time talking and reading to your child in your home language – it's an important part of who they are.
- Show a positive attitude towards the second language – you could even try learning it with your child.
- Provide books in both languages (try the library or the internet) and look out for dual-language books that you can read together.
- Buy, or borrow, book and CD sets in the second language so your child can listen to a story and follow the text.
- Ask children to tell you about their school work and about books they're reading in their second language.

Literacy difficulties

It's natural to be concerned if your child seems to be having problems with reading and writing. For whatever reason, some children find reading very difficult at first, while others may be reluctant to read at all. A few will have specific disabilities or learning difficulties which need specialist help. It may take some children a little longer than others, but the vast majority do learn to read in the end.

Reluctant readers

It can be frustrating trying to help a child who has no interest in reading and tries to avoid it at all costs, but do try to stay calm. If reading becomes a battleground, children are even less likely to want to pick up a book. Bear in mind that your child may be reluctant because they find reading difficult. Focus on building their confidence and on making reading fun. Here are a few ideas to try:

- Continue reading aloud to your child and try sharing the reading by taking turns or playing different characters.
- Suggest books that will appeal to your child's interests and sense of humour – not ones you think they should read.
- Provide a range of non-book reading material (see page 72 for some ideas).
- Let children choose what to read and don't be critical of their choice.
- Buy games or activities with simple instructions, so children have a reason to read.
- Encourage your child to read to younger members of the family.

Struggling readers

Children vary enormously in the time it takes them to learn to read. Some may be reading fluently at five or even younger, while others might still be struggling at seven or eight. Try not to compare your child's progress to that of their friends – even if other children seem to be progressing faster, it doesn't necessarily mean your child has a reading difficulty. Nor does it mean your child is unintelligent – many children who are of above-average intelligence still struggle with reading. Below are a few ways to help children who may be finding reading hard.

- Encourage your child to read to you every day – little and often works best.
- Spend time talking about a book and looking at the pictures together before your child tries to read it.
- Be aware of your child's level, but try to avoid suggesting books they might see as 'babyish.'
- Share the reading by taking turns.
- Play alphabet games, letter-sound games and word games together.

Remember to stay positive – sometimes your patience and encouragement may be all that is needed to help your child.

What happens at school?

Children are normally assessed when they start school and teachers will be looking out for important pre-reading skills, such as recognizing a few letter shapes and being able to hear letter sounds. If your child has difficulty with these things, it should be spotted during their first few terms at school and they may be given extra help. Children are monitored and assessed throughout their years at school, and those who are still struggling to read during their third year at school should be receiving extra support.

It's important to keep in contact with the school, so you can find out how your child is progressing. If you are worried that your child is struggling, you may want to make an appointment to see their teacher.

Before meeting your child's teacher, it might be helpful to jot down your concerns and make a note of any specific problems you've noticed. Here are a few things to look out for:

Does your child...

- confuse letters, such as 'b' and 'd', beyond the age of seven?
- have trouble sounding out and blending words?
- miss out or add words when reading?
- lose their place on the page or read a line twice?
- lack concentration while reading?
- have difficulty remembering or summarizing what they've read?
- often spell words using the right letters, but in the wrong order?

Getting support

When you meet your child's teacher, make sure you express all your concerns and observations, and let the teacher know about anything that might be affecting your child's ability to learn, such as ill health or changes in your home situation.

Ask what you can do to help, keep a note of any suggestions the teacher makes and find out if your child needs any extra support from the school. The teacher might suggest that your child has extra lessons with the school's literacy co-ordinator or special educational needs co-ordinator. If this happens, you should be sent regular updates on their progress.

Many children need a little extra help at some point – this doesn't mean that your child has a learning difficulty.

If children get support early on, it can prevent more serious problems from developing later.

If all else fails...

If, by the age of seven or eight, despite the school's best efforts, your child is still having serious difficulties with their reading, you can ask for them to be referred to an educational psychologist. Your child's school may be able to arrange this for you, but you might have to organize it privately yourself.

Special needs

Some children may have a disability or a specific learning difficulty which makes it harder for them to learn to read and write. For these children, expert diagnosis is essential, along with a teaching programme that has been designed specially for them. There are also lots of organizations and groups which offer support, ideas and advice. You can ask healthcare professionals how to contact both national and local groups, or go to the Usborne Quicklinks Website (see page 84) for links to sites which you may find useful.

Dyslexia

Dyslexia is a specific learning difficulty which causes problems with learning to read. Most dyslexic children seem to have difficulty identifying the sounds in words, so they struggle with playing sound games and learning the sounds of letters. Dyslexia affects around five to eight per cent of children, but it does tend to run in families. Schools are getting much better at identifying dyslexic children, but if you know that you or a relative have dyslexic difficulties, it's important to let your child's teacher know.

Dyslexic children do learn to read and write, but they need very careful help.

Dyspraxia

Dyspraxia shows itself in a variety of ways. A dyspraxic child may be slow to talk and their speech may be hard to understand. They may suffer from co-ordination problems, a short concentration span or poor listening skills. Dyspraxia can affect handwriting, reading and spelling, and may require more than one specialist to help deal with the different symptoms. It needs to be diagnosed by a doctor or a children's occupational therapist.

Hearing impairments

Even a mild hearing impairment can make it hard for a child to hear quiet speech sounds, such as 's', 'f' and 't'. Children with a hearing impairment will find it more difficult to learn the letter sounds, but – with specialist help – it can be done. Make sure your child's hearing tests are up to date and if you are concerned, talk to a healthcare professional.

Visual impairments

If your child often complains of headaches or has to hold a book very close to, or far from, their face to read it, it's a good idea to get their eyes tested. Wearing glasses may solve the problem. For children with a more serious visual impairment, many books are available in large print, Braille or as audio books, but you may need professional advice to make sure your child gets the help they need.

Other special needs

There are many other conditions which can affect a child's ability to read and write, such as Attention Deficit Disorder (ADD), Attention Deficit with Hyperactivity Disorder (ADHD), Autistic Spectrum Disorder (ASD) and a range of speech and language disorders. For links to helpful websites, go to the Usborne Quicklinks Website (see page 84).

Further help

If you need further information or advice about your child's language development, reading or writing, there are plenty of people and organizations you can turn to.

Literacy organizations are a good place to start. These offer a wealth of information on all aspects of literacy, including language development, reading aloud, choosing books, phonics, spelling, grammar and handwriting. There are links to organizations on the Usborne Quicklinks Website (see right).

Health visitors work closely with doctors and teachers, and specialize in healthcare, parenting and child development. Along with your child's teacher, they are an important first contact if you are concerned about any health issues affecting your child's literacy.

Your local library will have a range of useful information for parents, including details of preschool groups in your area, and the librarian can advise you on choosing books for your child. School library associations, literacy organizations and book-related websites publish lists of recommended children's books which may also be helpful (see the Usborne Quicklinks Website for links to useful sites).

Internet links

The internet is a great source of information for parents and carers. At the Usborne Quicklinks Website there are links to lots of useful websites, as well as suggestions for additional activities and puzzles to print out. To visit the sites, go to **www.usborne-quicklinks.com** and type the keywords 'read and write'.

Here are some of the things you can find via Usborne Quicklinks:

- Songs, rhymes and tongue twisters to share with children
- Activities, such as maze puzzles and word searches, to print out and try
- Online games where children can have fun with letters and sounds
- A phoneme pronunciation guide you can listen to
- Lists of suitable words for using in phonics activities
- Websites offering advice about children with special needs

Internet safety

The websites recommended in Usborne Quicklinks are regularly reviewed, but the content of a website may change at any time and Usborne Publishing is not responsible for the content or availability of websites other than its own.

Literacy development

Children don't just suddenly become readers and writers when they start school – the journey to literacy begins at birth and lasts a lifetime. Babies, toddlers and preschoolers need to develop a whole range of skills to prepare them for learning to read and write and the journey continues throughout a child's school career and beyond. It takes years to be able to read fluently and spell accurately – even well-read adults sometimes come across words they don't recognize or can't spell.

Reading levels

As your child's reading develops, one way of finding books at the right level is to look for those graded according to a readability measure, such as the Lexile scale. With this system, books are given a grade that shows how easy or difficult they are. Children are assessed to find their starting point on the scale and can then choose books that exactly match their level. There is more information about Lexiles on the Usborne Quicklinks Website (see opposite page).

Alternatively, some children's books now have a suggested age range printed on them to make it easier to choose suitable books.

Development charts

The following four pages show you some of the main things children learn and enjoy at different stages on their way to becoming readers and writers. Do remember, though, that these are only guidelines. No two children are exactly the same – they each develop at a different rate, learning new skills in their own time. Try not to compare your child to others and don't worry if they seem to be later at doing something than is suggested here.

The information on the following pages covers children's language and literacy development from birth to age 11 in the areas outlined below. (Language development is covered only up to the age of five. By this stage, a child's knowledge of how sentences are put together is much the same as an adult's, though their vocabulary continues to increase.)

Language development
This is about what children can hear, say and understand. It forms the basis for reading and writing.

Pre-reading or reading skills
This covers skills and experiences related to reading. Pre-reading skills are those that prepare children for reading.

Pre-writing or writing skills
This covers skills and experiences related to writing. Pre-writing skills are those that prepare children for writing.

0 – 2 years

Language development: Babies communicate through smiling, pointing and cooing, and babble their first speech-like sounds, such as 'babababa', at around eight months. They usually say their first meaningful words at around 10 to 14 months. By 18 months, they may be using as many as 50 words and will point when asked simple 'Where?' questions. From 18 to 24 months, they begin to say two-word phrases, such as 'mummy shoe'.

Pre-reading skills: Babies will listen to your voice as you sing nursery rhymes and they enjoy playing with, exploring and sharing books. Toddlers love to hear their favourite books again and again, and like to turn the pages. They can clap along and join in with simple action rhymes.

Pre-writing skills: Babies reach out for toys and move them from hand to hand by six months. At 12 months, they can pick up crumbs between their thumb and index finger, and like making finger patterns in spilt food. From 18 months, toddlers can hold a chunky crayon in either hand and can scribble to and fro, later adding lots of dots.

2 – 3 years

Language development: Children begin to use three-word sentences, such as 'Sam like car', and later add a fourth word, for example 'Sam like red car'. They understand two-part requests, such as 'Put your cup on the table', and later those with three parts, for example 'Put your cup on the table and find your shoes.' They ask lots of 'What?' and 'Who?' questions.

Pre-reading skills: Children continue to ask for their favourite books over and over again. They enjoy stories with rhymes and repeated phrases, and realize that the text, as well as the pictures, tells the story. They sometimes imitate reading-like behaviour, such as holding a book and turning the pages, and they may recognize the first letter of their name.

Pre-writing skills: Children use felt-tip pens, pencils, crayons and a computer mouse with more control. Using either hand, or one preferred hand, they make vertical and horizontal marks and large circular scribbles. They may sometimes pretend that they are 'writing'.

3 – 4 years

Language development: Children's language is more complex and confident, as they now talk in longer sentences and start linking sentences together. They can talk about present, past and future events. Their vocabulary grows rapidly, as they learn about 50 to 70 new words every week. They ask lots of 'Why?' and 'Where?' questions.

Pre-reading skills: Children enjoy longer stories and start to become familiar with storybook language, such as 'Once upon a time...' They predict what might happen in a story and can recall the main event. They can pick out the first sound in a word and may learn the sounds that some letters make. They begin to take an interest in print they see around them, and can hold a book the right way up and turn the pages.

Pre-writing skills: Children now have reasonable pencil control and may form letter-like shapes and some recognizable letters. They may attempt to trace or copy their own name, later trying to write it independently. They are increasingly aware that information can be given in writing.

4 – 5 years

Language development: Children can understand and use longer, more complex sentences and continue to learn lots of new words. They may still make a few errors with irregular words, such as 'buyed' instead of 'bought'. They take turns in longer conversations and ask the meaning of words they don't understand, as well as asking more 'When?' and 'How?' questions.

Reading skills: Children learn to sound out and name the letters of the alphabet. They begin to read phonically regular words by blending the letter sounds from left to right and start to recognize common irregular words, such as 'the', 'was' and 'are'. They read aloud slowly word by word. They like being read to from picture books and 'chapter books' with increasingly sophisticated storylines, and can talk about what they've listened to.

Writing skills: Children learn to form recognizable lower-case letters and can write their name. They use their phonics skills to write simple, regular three-letter words and learn to memorize tricky words, such as 'to', 'the' and 'of'. They invent spellings for most words, based on how they sound.

5 – 6 years

Reading skills: Children recognize consonant blends, such as 'spot' and 'frog', and learn that letters, or groups of letters, can be pronounced in different ways, such as 'cow' and 'blow'. They recognize regular and common irregular words that they've seen many times before and can use their phonics skills to work out unfamiliar regular words. They read aloud with more understanding and expression, pausing at the end of sentences. They still like to be read to from books beyond their reading level, enjoying illustrated 'chapter books' and information books on their favourite topics.

Writing skills: Children now refer to the letters of the alphabet by name. The letters are mostly correctly formed and facing the right way. Children begin to plan and write simple sentences independently, using a capital letter at the start, a full stop at the end and proper spacing between words. They still spell words as they sound, with a combination of regular spelling and invented spelling. They begin to recognize that some words sound the same but have different spellings, such as 'too', 'to' and 'two'.

6 – 7 years

Reading skills: Many children are now reading silently and independently. Their reading aloud is increasingly fluent and expressive, though they still hesitate over unfamiliar words. Occasionally, they may read one word for another, but often spot their mistake when it doesn't make sense. Their sight vocabulary is growing and they start to break down longer, unfamiliar words into syllables, shorter words or word parts. They still like being read to, but also enjoy reading, and re-reading, 'chapter books' and information books on their own. They may skim-read a few pages before choosing a book.

Writing skills: Handwriting is usually quite regular, with letters facing the right way. Children are more aware of the correct way to spell words and use their knowledge of vocabulary and spelling patterns to tackle tricky or longer words where they can. When unsure, they spell words how they sound. They think carefully about what they want to write and are more creative about presentation. They begin to use commas to separate items in a list and may use question marks. They learn to re-read what they have written, checking for spellings, capital letters and basic punctuation.

7 – 9 years

Reading skills: Children now read aloud with greater fluency and expression, and read silently at an even faster pace. They recognize many everyday words automatically and work out unfamiliar words by spotting known letter sequences, word parts and words within words. If a sentence doesn't make sense, they re-read it. They enjoy reading longer 'chapter books', comics, magazines and special-interest books, and begin to use indexes, glossaries, dictionaries and computers to find information.

Writing skills: Children use joined-up writing and begin to write with a pen. Most common words are spelled correctly – including familiar irregular words – while others are tackled using known spelling patterns, word parts and phonics skills. They begin to use a dictionary to look up spellings. Children learn how to plan, compose and proofread their work. Their sentences are longer and more interesting, with basic punctuation in place. They begin to use question marks, apostrophes, exclamation marks and speech marks, and their writing may be arranged in paragraphs.

9 – 11 years

Reading skills: By now, most everyday words are recognized automatically and those that aren't can be worked out using phonics skills and knowledge of spelling patterns. Children read more extensively and may enjoy increasingly lengthy and complex fiction. They often have definite reading preferences and may have a favourite author. They begin to 'read between the lines' to discover the deeper meaning of a book or article, thinking about themes, characters and points of view. They learn how to discuss texts, expressing their opinions and referring back to the text to support them.

Writing skills: Children develop their own style of handwriting and may use a range of computer software to present their writing. They spell familiar words correctly and use various strategies to attempt unfamiliar or irregular words, including greater use of dictionaries and computer spellcheckers. Children learn how to edit their own writing to make improvements and amend punctuation to clarify meaning. They experiment with different forms of writing, such as reports, letters and instructions, and realize that some kinds of writing need to be more formal than others.

Phoneme chart

This chart shows the 44 phonemes of the English language and the ways they're most commonly spelled. The phonemes shown here are based on standard English pronunciation, so some of them may be pronounced slightly differently in different regional accents. You can hear the standard pronunciations on the Usborne Quicklinks Website (see page 84).

Phoneme*	Graphemes	Examples
/a/	a	apple, bat
/b/	b, bb	ball, cabbage
/d/	d, dd, -ed	doll, teddy, called
/e/	e, ea	bed, bread
/f/	f, ff, ph, gh	fox, huff, phone, tough
/g/	g, gg	gas, digger
/h/	h	hat
/i/	i, y	it, symbol
/j/	j, g, ge, dge	jam, giraffe, large, hedge
/k/	c, k, ck	cap, king, luck
/l/	l, ll	log, well
/m/	m, mm, mb	mop, mummy, comb
/n/	n, nn, gn, kn	nut, sunny, gnome, knit
/o/	o, a (after w)	dog, wash
/p/	p, pp	pet, puppy
/r/	r, rr, wr	run, parrot, wrap
/s/	s, ss, c, sc	sit, hiss, city, scenic
/t/	t, tt, -ed	tip, letter, bumped
/u/	u, o	plug, money
/v/	v, ve	vet, give
/w/	w, wh	web, whale
/y/	y	yellow
/z/	z, zz, se, ze, s	zoo, fizz, tease, sneeze, his

* The letter 'c' isn't shown because it shares the same phoneme as 'k'.
The letter 'q' isn't shown because its sound is made up of two other phonemes: /k/ and /w/.
The letter 'x' is a combination of the two phonemes /k/ and /s/.

Phoneme	Graphemes	Examples
/ch/	ch, tch	chat, fetch
/ng/	ng, n (before k)	sing, think
/sh/	sh, ss (before -ion and -ure),	ship, permission, pressure
	t (before -ion and -ial),	nation, partial,
	c (before -ian, -ious and -ial)	magician, precious, special
/th/ (unvoiced)*	th	thick
/th/ (voiced)*	th	that
/zh/	s (before -ion and -ure)	television, treasure
/ai/	ai, ay, a-e, eigh, ey	train, say, cake, sleigh, grey
/air/	air, are, ear	stair, hare, pear
/ar/	ar, a	arm, rather
/ear/	ear, eer, ere	fear, beer, here
/ee/	ee, ea, ie, y, ey	street, heat, thief, happy, honey
/er/	-er, -ar, -or,	sister, cellar, tutor,
	-our, -re, -ure,	colour, metre, adventure,
	a, e, i, o, u	above, sudden, horrible, octopus, upon
/igh/	igh, ie, i-e, y, i	right, pie, bike, by, kind
/oa/	oa, ow, oe, o-e, o	soap, tow, foe, bone, so
/oi/	oi, oy	oil, toy
/oo/ [long]	oo, ew, ue, u-e, ou	moon, blew, clue, June, group
/oo/ [short]	oo, u, oul	book, put, would
/or/	or, aw, au, ore,	fork, claw, pause, core,
	al, oor, oar	walk, door, soar
/ow/	ow, ou	how, hound
/ur/	ur, er, ir, ear, or (after w)	curl, her, bird, earn, worm
/ure/	ure, oor, our	sure, poor, detour

* An 'unvoiced' sound is made just by forcing air between your lips, teeth or tongue, e.g. /f/, /t/ and /th/ (as in 'thin') are unvoiced sounds. To make a 'voiced' sound, you also use your vocal cords, e.g. /v/, /d/ and /th/ (as in 'then') are voiced sounds.

Letter formation chart

There are a number of slightly different handwriting styles for teaching to children, but the one shown here is the most common (the white dot shows where to start each letter). It's worth finding out which style is taught at your child's school, so you can use the same one at home.

Glossary

alliteration A sequence of words starting with the same sound, e.g. 'crunchy carrots'.

auditory memory The ability to remember what you have heard.

blending Running two or more sounds together to read a word, e.g. running the sounds /d/ /o/ /g/ together to make 'dog'.

consonant Any letter of the alphabet except for 'a', 'e', 'i', 'o' or 'u'.

consonant blend Two or more separate consonant sounds that are blended together, e.g. 'sl' in 'slip' and 'str' in 'strip'.

decodable book A book mostly made up of phonically regular words.

decoding Translating written letters into spoken words.

digraph A two-letter grapheme that represents a single sound in a word, e.g. 'sh', 'th', 'oo' and 'ee'.

fine motor skills Precise movements, for example of the hands and fingers, such as those needed for controlling a pencil.

fluent reading The ability to read smoothly and expressively without hesitation.

grapheme A letter, or group of letters, that represents a single sound in a word, e.g. 's', 'ch', 'igh' and 'eigh'.

invented spelling Making up spellings based on how words sound.

irregular words (tricky words) Words that aren't spelled exactly as they sound. 'One' and 'two' are irregular words.

phoneme A single sound within a word. The word 'ship' has three phonemes – /sh/ /i/ /p/.

phonics A way of teaching reading that focuses on the link between written letters and the sounds they represent.

prefix A letter, or group of letters, at the beginning of a word that changes the word's meaning, e.g. 'un' + 'happy' ('unhappy').

print awareness Knowing about print, what it looks like, what it's for and how it works.

regular words Words that are spelled exactly as they sound. 'Sit', 'chop' and 'jumps' are regular words.

segmenting Breaking a word down into its individual sounds to spell it.

sight words Words that you recognize automatically as soon as you see them.

sounding out Saying the sounds of the letters in a word, one by one from left to right.

suffix A letter, or group of letters, at the end of a word that changes the way the word is used, e.g. 'quick' + 'ly' ('quickly').

syllable A word part that contains a vowel or vowel sound such as 'y'. The word 'map' has one syllable; the word 'dus-ty' has two.

synthetic phonics A method of teaching reading where children learn to sound out letters and run them together to read words. They also learn to break words down into their separate sounds to spell them.

tripod grip A way of holding a pencil or pen with the thumb, index finger and middle finger positioned near the tip (see page 42).

vowel Any of the letters 'a', 'e', 'i', 'o' or 'u'. The letter 'y' sometimes works like a vowel in words such as 'symbol'.

Index

With thanks to...

Emma and Katie for inspiration; Molly, Jess, Becky and Yasmin; Brendan and Grace Malliagh; Mrs Cockle and her wonderful class at Long Ditton Infant and Nursery School; Emma Helbrough for indexing; Sam Taplin for proofreading; Jessica Greenwell for proofreading and website research

Photo credits:

The publishers are grateful to the following for permission to reproduce material: p8 © Eric Audras/Getty Images; p22 © JUPITERIMAGES/Liz Banfield; p30 © Michael Goldman/Getty Images; p40 © Jean Louis Batt/Getty Images; p41 © Andersen Ross/Getty Images; p73 © Blend Images/Alamy; p77 © PhotoAlto/Alamy

Additional illustrations: Dubravka Kolanovic

Additional photography: Graham Alder at MMStudios

Digital imaging: Keith Furnival

First published in 2008 by Usborne Publishing Ltd., Usborne House, 83–85 Saffron Hill, London EC1N 8RT, England. www.usborne.com